READING/WRITING COMPANION

COVER: James Haskins

mheducation.com/prek-12

Send all inquiries to:
McGraw-Hill Education
Two Penn Plaza
New York, New York 10121

ISBN: 978-0-07-700891-8
MHID: 0-07-700891-X

Printed in the United States of America.

9 LMN 24 23   B

Welcome to Wonders !

Read exciting **Literature**, **Science**, and **Social Studies** texts!

★ **LEARN** about the world around you!

★ **THINK**, **SPEAK**, and **WRITE** about genres!

★ **COLLABORATE** in discussion and inquiry!

★ **EXPRESS** yourself!

my.mheducation.com
Use your student login to read core texts, practice grammar and spelling, explore research projects and more!

UNIT 3

GENRE STUDY 1 **REALISTIC FICTION**

GENRE STUDY 2 **NARRATIVE NONFICTION**

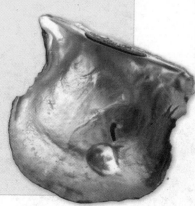

Cindy Miller Hopkins/DanitaDelimont.com/Newscom

GENRE STUDY **3 ARGUMENTATIVE TEXT**

WRAP UP THE UNIT

Digital Tools Find this eBook and other resources at **my.mheducation.com**

GENRE STUDY 1 **BIOGRAPHY**

GENRE STUDY 2 **DRAMA**

GENRE STUDY 3 POETRY

WRAP UP THE UNIT

SOCIAL STUDIES

 Digital Tools Find this eBook and other resources at **my.mheducation.com**

Ken Cavanagh/McGraw-Hill Education

Talk About It

Talk About It

Essential Question

What kinds of challenges transform people?

COLLABORATE

Rock climbing can be an enjoyable challenge. Persistent practice is important in mastering difficult climbing skills. There is a lot to learn. However, mastering a climbing skill is like solving a dilemma. It can make you feel great!

Talk to a partner about why rock climbing and other challenges might be transforming experiences. Write your ideas in the web.

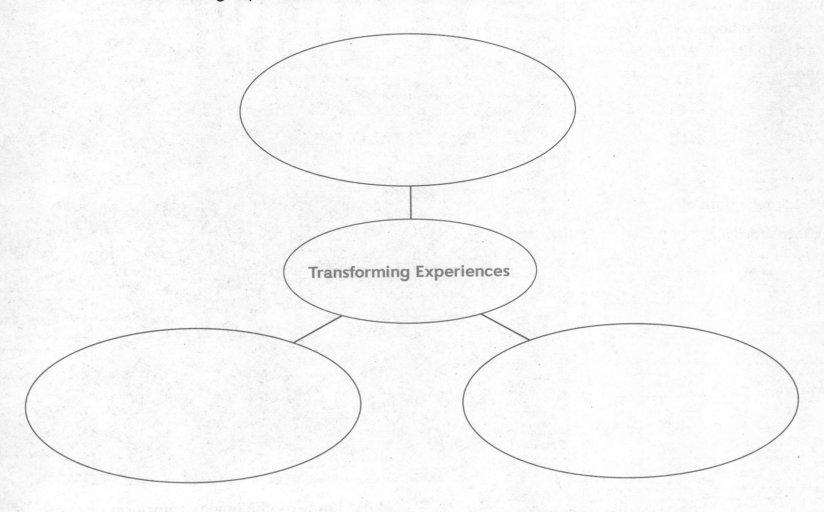

Transforming Experiences

BLAST BACK! studysync

Go online to **my.mheducation.com** and read the "Up to the Challenge" Blast. Think about how facing challenges affects people. What are some ways people are transformed by challenges? Then blast back your response.

Celin Serbo/Aurora Photos

TAKE NOTES

To help you focus as you read, set a purpose for reading. Preview the title and illustrations. What questions do you hope will be answered in the text? Write your ideas here.

_____

_____

_____

_____

As you read, take note of

Interesting Words _____

_____

_____

_____

_____

Key Details _____

_____

_____

_____

_____

_____

Facing the STORM

Steve Cieslawski

Essential Question

?

What kinds of challenges transform people?

Read how a severe weather threat transforms a shy and timid girl.

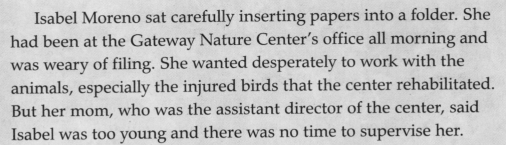

Isabel Moreno sat carefully inserting papers into a folder. She had been at the Gateway Nature Center's office all morning and was weary of filing. She wanted desperately to work with the animals, especially the injured birds that the center rehabilitated. But her mom, who was the assistant director of the center, said Isabel was too young and there was no time to supervise her.

"I've been a weekend volunteer this whole school year," Isabel thought. "I know more about birds than almost anyone here," she said to herself with conviction, recalling as evidence the extensive research she had done reading books and web sites on natural history. Then she sighed. She had never been good at speaking up for herself, and who would listen to a shy seventh grader anyway?

Suddenly, the quiet was shattered by Amy Jensen bursting in and letting the door slam. Isabel felt herself shrink. Amy, who had been a volunteer a bit longer than Isabel, was 16 and strutted around like she owned the place. "Hey, Isabel, I've got a job for you," she barked, planting a hand on Isabel's shoulder.

Isabel **recoiled** from Amy's touch, but she willed herself to remain still. "Don't make trouble," she reminded herself, though she would have loved to brush Amy's hand off. "I have to finish this filing," she squeaked **feebly**.

Just then, Isabel's mother rushed into the room with Mr. Garza, the custodian. "The hurricane forecast for Miami has **skewed** to the south and is entering the Gulf," Mrs. Moreno reported. "We should be okay up here in the inlet, but we'll likely get some fierce and **persistent** winds. I've sent the other volunteers home, but I need you girls to help Mr. Garza get the storm shutters down in here and in the aviary. Then I'll take you home." Isabel leaped to her feet, excited to have an opportunity to help the birds.

FIND TEXT EVIDENCE

Read

Paragraphs 1–4
Point of View

Whose thoughts does the text show? **Underline** examples. What does this tell you about the point of view, or perspective, in the story so far?

_____

_____

Paragraph 5
Make Predictions

What do you think Isabel will do later in the story? **Draw a box** around text you used to make that prediction.

_____

_____

Reread

Author's Craft

How does the author make it clear that Isabel is afraid to speak up?

FIND TEXT EVIDENCE

Read

Paragraphs 1–2
Context Clues

Circle context clues that help you determine the correct meaning of the multiple-meaning word *batter* in paragraph 2. Write the intended meaning.

_____

_____

Paragraphs 3–4
Theme

Underline text that describes Amy's reaction to the storm. What does this help you infer about her?

_____

_____

_____

Reread

Author's Craft

How does Amy's reaction to the storm help the author reveal more about Isabel?

Mrs. Moreno's cell phone jangled, and she answered it at once, listening intently. "Change of plans," she announced as she hung up. "The winds are worse than expected along the coastline, so the Gulf Shore Preserve needs help preparing for the storm. I've got to go down there with the staff. We'll take the inlet bridge, so we shouldn't be gone long. Stay inside with Mr. Garza after you get the storm shutters down. And call me on my cell if there are any problems," she directed as she dashed out.

Amy crowed that she was now "in charge." Isabel groaned inwardly, but said nothing. Mr. Garza and the girls worked quickly and were soon back inside, listening to the wind batter and rattle the shutters. When Mr. Garza found an emergency weather report on the computer, a worried expression crossed his face. "A storm surge is heading our way, right up the inlet," he announced. "We're in for some flooding."

Authoritative as ever, Amy called Isabel's mother to tell her the news, but she sounded flustered when she hung up. "The surge has flooded the bridge, and they're stuck there!" she gasped. "What do we do?"

Isabel was unnerved that both Mr. Garza and Amy seemed so panicked, but after silently considering the **dilemma** for a few seconds, she **roused** herself and said calmly, "We should move the birds to the reptile house. It's on higher ground." As she strode out of the building with Mr. Garza and Amy following, she caught a glimpse of the satellite image on the computer. The **vastness** of the storm nearly filled the entire Gulf now.

Once inside the aviary, Isabel watched Amy lunge from cage to cage, agitating the birds. "Don't jump around so much!" Isabel instructed. "They're scared enough as it is, and your sudden movements aren't helping." Amy meekly calmed down, but she was shaking.

"Just think about the birds," Isabel said as they carried each cage up to the reptile house. The hawks screeched and beat their wings when they felt the wind. Isabel spoke soothingly to them, and they soon grew calmer. Amy watched in awe and tried to mimic Isabel's tone. Just as the water in the bird house had risen to their shins, they finished relocating the birds and waited inside the reptile house for the storm to subside.

After several hours, the water had receded, and Mrs. Moreno was able to return to the center. She expressed concern that she'd left them alone for so long, but Mr. Garza reassured her that Isabel's foresight and cool thinking had saved the birds.

Mrs. Moreno gazed at her daughter admiringly. "How did you **summon** such confidence and courage?" she asked Isabel.

"I'm not sure," Isabel admitted. "All I could think about was how scared the birds must have felt in their cages, and I just took charge."

"I'm proud of you, Isabel," said Mrs. Moreno.

Isabel paused a second. "I guess I'm proud of myself, Mom!"

Steve Cieslawski

Summarize

Use your notes to write a summary about what happens in the story and how Isabel changes.

FIND TEXT EVIDENCE 🔍

Read

Paragraphs 1–2
Make Predictions

How accurate was the prediction you made on page 3? **Underline** text evidence that supports your response.

_____

_____

Paragraphs 3–7
Theme

How has Isabel changed from the beginning of the story? Explain.

_____

_____

_____

_____

Reread

Author's Craft

How does the author's use of description help you visualize the scene inside the aviary?

Vocabulary

Use the example sentences to talk with a partner about each word. Then answer the questions.

dilemma

Joe faced a **dilemma** when he couldn't decide which puppy to take home.

Describe a dilemma you have faced.

_____

_____

_____

feebly

The weak, newborn pony **feebly** tried to stand.

When might a person do something feebly?

_____

_____

_____

persistent

My baby sister's **persistent** crying keeps everyone up at night.

What persistent sounds are heard in your neighborhood?

_____

_____

recoiled

Hudson **recoiled** from the needle when it was time to get his booster shot.

Describe a time when you recoiled from something.

_____

_____

roused

The alarm clock **roused** the girl from a deep sleep.

How are you roused from sleep in the morning?

_____

_____

 Build Your Word List Pick a word you found interesting in the selection you read. Make a word web of different forms of the word in your writer's notebook.

skewed

The line **skewed** to the right because I did not use a straight edge to draw it.

How are the meanings of *skewed* and *swerved* similar?

_____

_____

_____

summon

I was able to **summon** a burst of energy and win the race.

When might you need to summon a burst of energy?

_____

_____

_____

vastness

The **vastness** of the crowd made it hard for me to find my friends.

What is a synonym of *vastness*?

_____

_____

Context Clues

Words in a story can have more than one possible meaning. To figure out which meaning is correct, look for context clues within the paragraph that contains the multiple-meaning word.

🔍 FIND TEXT EVIDENCE

I see the word filing *below. I know this word can mean "smoothing and shaping with a tool" or "putting papers away." The paragraph says Isabel is "inserting papers into a folder" in an office, so I know the second meaning is correct.*

Isabel Moreno sat carefully inserting papers into a folder. She had been at the Gateway Nature Center's office all morning and was weary of filing.

Your Turn Use context clues to determine the correct meanings of these words as they are used in "Facing the Storm."

staff, *page 4* _____

_____

tone, *page 5* _____

_____

Make Predictions

When reading realistic fiction, use what you know about the ways the characters act to predict what they might do next. Then use text evidence to **confirm** or **revise** your predictions as you read on.

 FIND TEXT EVIDENCE

After you read page 4 of "Facing the Storm," you may have used what you know about the characters to predict how Isabel and Amy would react to the approaching storm. Reread to confirm or revise your prediction.

Page 4

Authoritative as ever, Amy called Isabel's mother to tell her the news, but she sounded flustered when she hung up. "The surge has flooded the bridge, and they're stuck there!" she gasped. "What do we do?"

On page 3, Amy tells Isabel, "I've got a job for you." I predicted Amy would give Isabel orders during the storm. Then I read that Amy "sounded flustered" when she heard Mrs. Moreno was stuck on the bridge, so I revised my prediction.

 Your Turn What prediction did you make about what would happen after Amy became flustered? Tell how you confirmed or revised that prediction.

_____

_____

_____

_____

_____

Point of View

Point of view refers to the identity of the narrator. In the realistic fiction piece "Facing the Storm," the story is told in third-person limited point of view. In third-person limited, the narrator knows the thoughts and feelings of only one character. The narrator in "Facing the Storm" uses strong, vivid verbs, which is a common feature of realistic fiction.

FIND TEXT EVIDENCE

Phrases such as "wanted desperately" and "felt herself shrink" indicate that "Facing the Storm" is told mostly from Isabel's perspective. The author's use of vivid verbs, such as shattered, bursting, *and* strutted, *helps me visualize the characters' actions.*

Here are some other points of view used in fiction: **First person:** The narrator is a character in the story and uses the pronouns *I, we, us,* and *our.* **Third-person omniscient (or all-knowing):** The narrator is not in the story. The narrator knows the thoughts and feelings of all characters and uses the pronouns *he, she,* and *they.*

Page 4

Mrs. Moreno's cell phone jangled, and she answered it at once, listening intently. "Change of plans," she announced as she hung up. "The winds are worse than expected along the coastline, so the Gulf Shore Preserve needs help preparing for the storm. I've got to go down there with the staff. We'll take the inlet bridge, so we shouldn't be gone long. Stay inside with Mr. Garza after you get the storm shutters down. And call me on my cell if there are any problems," she directed as she dashed out.

Amy crowed that she was now "in charge." Isabel groaned inwardly, but said nothing. Mr. Garza and the girls worked quickly and were soon back inside, listening to the wind batter and rattle the shutters. When Mr. Garza found an emergency weather report on the computer, a worried expression crossed his face. "A storm surge is heading our way, right up the inlet," he announced. "We're in for some flooding."

Authoritative as ever, Amy called Isabel's mother to tell her the news, but she sounded flustered when she hung up. "The surge has flooded the bridge, and they're stuck there!" she gasped. "What do we do?"

Isabel was unnerved that both Mr. Garza and Amy seemed so panicked, but after silently considering the **dilemma** for a few seconds, she **roused** herself and said calmly, "We should move the birds to the reptile house. It's on higher ground." As she strode out of the building with Mr. Garza and Amy following, she caught a glimpse of the satellite image on the computer. The **vastness** of the storm nearly filled the entire Gulf now.

Third-Person Limited Point of View

The narrator presents events mainly through one character's point of view.

Strong, Vivid Verbs

Strong verbs give the reader a more vivid picture of the events.

COLLABORATE

Your Turn Choose a new example from page 4 that shows the story is told mainly from Isabel's point of view. Then identify two vivid verbs that help you visualize the action in the story.

_____

_____

_____

_____

Theme

Authors often use a central plot event to focus the reader's attention on a theme, or message, in a story. To identify a story's theme, use what you learn about the characters, conflicts, and events in the plot to consider what message or idea the author is trying to convey. Remember that stories may have multiple themes.

 FIND TEXT EVIDENCE

As I reread "Facing the Storm," I see that each of the characters is affected in a significant way by the hurricane. Thinking about how the characters react and change as a result of this central event will help me identify a theme of the story.

Detail
Shy Isabel feels frustrated that she doesn't get to work with the birds at the nature center.

↓

Detail
Normally bossy Amy is flustered as the storm approaches.

↓

Detail

↓

Theme

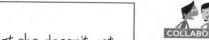 **Your Turn** Reread "Facing the Storm." Identify another key detail about how a character is affected by the plot and add it to the chart. Then state a theme of the story in the last box.

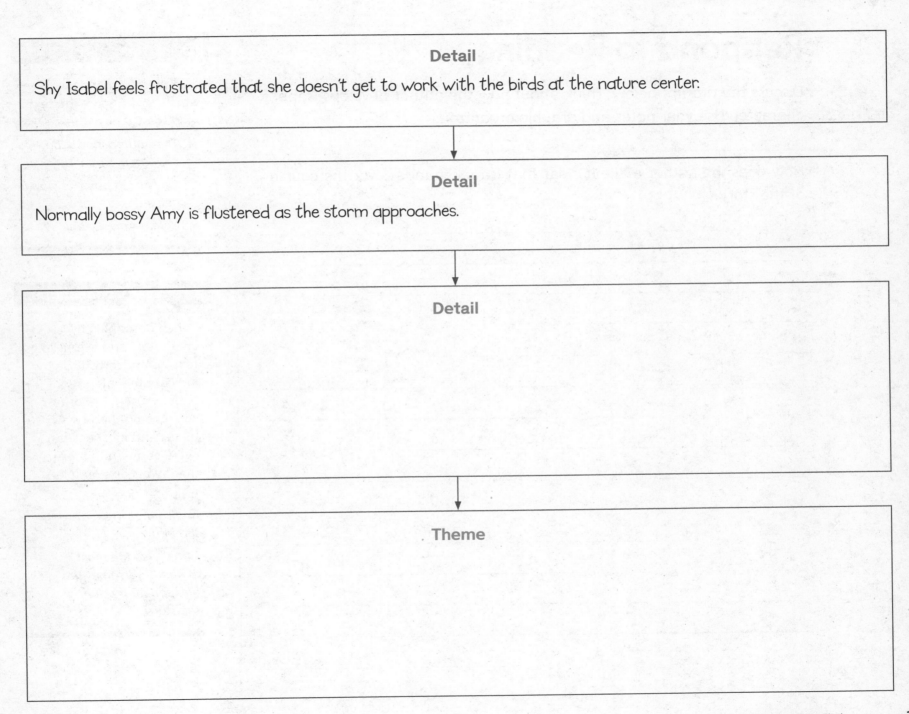

Detail

Shy Isabel feels frustrated that she doesn't get to work with the birds at the nature center.

Detail

Normally bossy Amy is flustered as the storm approaches.

Detail

Theme

Respond to Reading

COLLABORATE

Discuss the prompt below. Think about how the author develops Isabel's character. Use your notes and graphic organizer.

How does the author make it clear that Isabel changes over the course of the story?

_____

_____

_____

_____

_____

_____

_____

_____

_____

_____

_____

_____

_____

_____

_____

Quick Tip

Use these sentence starters to discuss the text and to organize ideas.

- *The author shows the change in Isabel by . . .*
- *The story's point of view helps the author . . .*
- *Unlike Amy, Isabel . . .*

Grammar Connections

When describing characters and events in a text, use adverbs to indicate the intensity of actions. Use *more* or *less* when comparing two things and *most* or *least* when comparing more than two. For example,

*Amy was **less** capable than Isabel when moving the birds.*

*Isabel was the **most** efficient person at the bird sanctuary during the storm.*

Identify and Gather Information

Before doing research on a topic, think about the questions you would like answered about the topic. This will help you identify what kind of information to look for and find relevant sources of information. Use these tips to identify and gather information:

- List questions you would like answered and sources that might give relevant information.
- Use the answers to your questions to create an outline of main points you will cover.
- Take notes on relevant information.
- Keep track of sources you used as well as those you might want to use later. Make sure to cite your sources.

What are some sources you might use to gather information?

_____

_____

_____

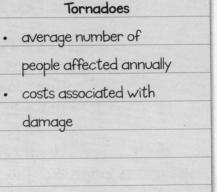

Tornadoes
• average number of people affected annually
• costs associated with damage

This list shows a student's notes about her main points. Add another possible note.

 Tech Tip

Consider software programs you may be able to use to design and create images for your poster.

COLLABORATE

Create a Poster With a partner, create a poster that details what to do in the case of one type of natural disaster, such as a tsunami, hurricane, or tornado. Consider these questions as you begin:

- What are potential effects of the disaster?
- What are the steps people can take to stay safe?

Discuss with your partner the types of visuals you will add to your poster, such as photographs, hand-drawn illustrations, or diagrams. After you complete your poster, you will share it with the class.

Lizzie Bright and the Buckminster Boy

Literature Anthology: pages 180–191

? **How does the author's use of personification help you visualize the setting as Turner rows the boat?**

Talk About It Reread the first paragraph on **Literature Anthology** page 186. Talk with a partner about what the author's descriptions help you picture in your mind.

Cite Text Evidence What two examples of personification help you visualize the setting? Use text evidence to describe the imagery.

Quick Tip

Personification is a type of figurative language. Personification gives human qualities to something that is nonhuman. Use the word *person* to help you remember the meaning of "personification."

Personification	What It Means	What I Visualize

Write I can visualize the setting because the author uses personification to

_____

_____

_____

 How does the author use descriptive language to show how Turner's attitude toward the whale changes?

To further explore the encounter between Turner and the whale, think about why he reaches out his hand toward the whale. Why do you think Turner tries to touch it?

COLLABORATE

Talk About It Reread **Literature Anthology** page 189. Talk with a partner about the way the author describes the encounter between Turner and the whale.

Cite Text Evidence What phrases help the reader understand Turner's experience with the whale and how this experience affected him? Write text evidence in the chart.

Text Evidence	What It Means

Write The author uses descriptive language to show how Turner changes

by _____

_____

How do you know that Turner's outlook has changed?

Talk About It Reread the last four paragraphs on **Literature Anthology** page 191. Talk with a partner about Turner's feelings at the end of the story.

Cite Text Evidence What clues show how Turner feels by the end of the story? Record text evidence in the chart.

Quick Tip

Think about how Turner felt before encountering the whales. What is different about the way he feels now? Use the illustration on pages 190–191 to help you understand how Turner has changed.

Text Evidence	Why It Is Important

Write I know that Turner's outlook has changed because the author _____

_____

_____

Respond to Reading

COLLABORATE

Discuss the prompt below. Consider how the author conveys Turner's thoughts and feelings. Use your notes and graphic organizer.

How does Gary D. Schmidt use Turner's encounter with the whale to help you understand the message in this story?

_____

_____

_____

_____

_____

_____

_____

_____

_____

_____

_____

_____

_____

_____

_____

Quick Tip

Use these sentence starters to talk about and cite text evidence.

Gary D. Schmidt introduces the whale . . .

It helps Turner . . .

This helps me understand that . . .

Self-Selected Reading

Choose a text and fill in your writer's notebook with the title, author, and genre of the selection. Include a personal response to the text in your writer's notebook. A personal response might include an experience of which the selection reminds you. It might also include how you feel about what you are reading.

Confronting a Challenge

Literature Anthology:
pages 194–195

1   When I finally told Ben I couldn't skate, he volunteered to teach me. Even though Ben was very patient, I was so embarrassed by my clumsiness that I began to make up more excuses for not skating.

2   About a month later, walking home from school, I discovered a faster route home. It took me past a large pond that was completely frozen over. One day I noticed a woman teaching a young girl to skate. The girl was attempting to jump and spin in the air. Over and over, she pushed off the ground with the toe of her skate. And over and over, she landed hard on the ice.

3   After I had been watching the girl practice for about a week, one Thursday afternoon she suddenly lifted off the ground, spun in the air, and landed on her feet! Her hard work and perseverance had paid off.

4   Later, alone in my bedroom, I started my social studies homework. I read a chapter in my textbook about Robert Peary and Matthew Henson who explored the Arctic together in 1909. I could only imagine the fears these explorers had to conquer in order to visit a remote region few people had ever traveled to before—a place much colder than Minnesota!

Reread paragraph 1. **Circle** why the narrator stopped skating. Write it here:

_____

_____

Now **underline** the clue in paragraph 3 that shows the narrator's attitude was changing.

COLLABORATE

Talk with a partner about why the narrator's attitude was changing. Then reread the fourth paragraph and **draw a box** around another thing that changed the narrator's attitude.

5   When I finished reading I made a pact with myself. The next day I used some money I had earned shoveling snow to buy myself some brand new skates. Every day on the way home from school I stopped at the pond, laced up, and wobbled onto the ice, right next to the figure skater who had landed her jump. As she perfected her twists and tricks, I taught myself to glide and turn. It was hard being a beginner, and when I fell I had to fight the urge to simply give up. Instead, every time I went down, I just picked myself up and started over again. If nothing else, I was persistent.

6   Soon I was able to keep my balance and skate more confidently. In just a few weeks, I was actually ready to practice the speed skating, fast stops, and quick turns needed for ice hockey. When I was finally ready to show Ben my newfound skating ability, he was impressed. He told me I should join the local hockey league.

7   I tried out and was chosen for a team. By the end of the season, not only was I part of a winning team, but also I had a group of new friends, including Ben.

In paragraph 5, **number** the steps the narrator takes to make a change. **Underline** words and phrases that show how he feels about the process.

Reread paragraph 6. How do you know that the narrator is not going to give up? **Circle** the text evidence.

COLLABORATE

Reread paragraph 7. Talk with a partner about how things have changed for the narrator. **Make a mark** in the margin beside the clue that helps support your discussion. Write it here:

_____

_____

_____

_____

? **How does the author show how the narrator changes from the beginning of the story to the end?**

Talk About It Reread the excerpts on pages 18 and 19. Talk with a partner about how the narrator changes from the first paragraph to the last.

Cite Text Evidence How does the author help you understand how the narrator changes? Record text evidence in the chart.

Quick Tip

Change in character is shown through the character's thoughts, words, actions, and how others treat them. Think about how the narrator feels in the beginning. How do you know these are his feelings? How do you know he is changing? Use text evidence to support your ideas.

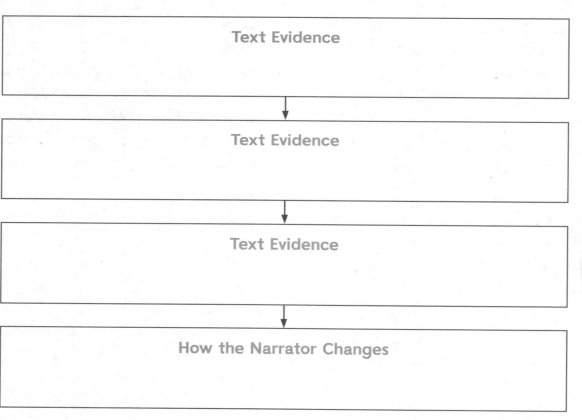

> Text Evidence
>
> ↓
>
> Text Evidence
>
> ↓
>
> Text Evidence
>
> ↓
>
> How the Narrator Changes

Write I know the narrator changes because the author _____

_____

Setting

A personal narrative describes events the author experienced. The **setting** is the time and place in which the events take place. Setting can contribute to the conflict, or problem, the narrator experiences. The author can use details of the setting to help develop the plot of a personal narrative.

FIND TEXT EVIDENCE

In the second paragraph on **Literature Anthology** page 194, the narrator contrasts the weather in Minnesota with that of his home state of California. The plot develops around the challenges the narrator faces as he tries to adapt to his new surroundings.

> Everything changed when my family moved to St. Paul, Minnesota, where the average winter temperature is around 10 degrees Fahrenheit.

Your Turn Reread the rest of Literature Anthology page 194. Then answer the questions below.

- Why does the Minnesota weather create a problem for the narrator?

_____

- Explain how the author uses an additional setting detail to help resolve the narrator's conflict. _____

_____

_____

When describing the setting of your personal narrative, think about what details will help you develop the plot. Consider how the setting's weather, location, and time period contribute to the narrative's conflict and resolution.

Text Connections

? **How does the photographer show the boys' relationship? How does this relationship compare to the ones in *Lizzie Bright and the Buckminster Boy* and "Confronting a Challenge"?**

Talk About It With a partner, discuss how each boy in the photograph is helping the other to overcome challenges. Compare the boys to Turner and the whale and the narrator and the figure skater.

Cite Text Evidence Look at the photograph. Work with a partner to find and **circle** clues that show how the interaction between the boys is benefiting them. List the ways in the margin beside the photograph.

Write The boys in the photograph are like Turner and the narrator because _____

_____

_____

_____

_____

_____

_____

_____

Quick Tip

To help you keep track of the benefits of all three relationships, create a three-column chart with the headings *Lizzie Bright and the Buckminster Boy*, "Confronting a Challenge," and Photo of Boys. Use the columns to list and compare the benefits of each interaction.

These sixth graders are part of their school's new One-on-One mentoring program. The program pairs two students with different talents who mentor and work together for one hour a week.

Present Your Work

COLLABORATE

Discuss how you will present your poster describing the steps people can take to stay safe during a natural disaster. Use the presenting checklist as you practice your presentation. Discuss the sentence starters below and write your answers.

One surprising safety tip I learned was _____

_____

_____

I would like to learn more about how to _____

_____

_____

✔ Presenting Checklist

☐ Define each partner's role in the presentation and rehearse it in advance.

☐ Present ideas using a logical and organized sequence that reflects your poster's content.

☐ Emphasize points so the audience can follow important ideas.

☐ Make appropriate eye contact with the audience.

☐ Speak loudly and clearly.

Denise McCullough

Expert Model

Literature Anthology: pages 180–191

Features of Realistic Fiction

Realistic fiction is a story about events that could happen in real life. Realistic fiction

- has a narrator who tells the story from a clear point of view;

- has well-developed characters who speak and behave realistically;

- has an engaging plot, or sequence of events.

Analyze an Expert Model Studying realistic fiction will help you write it on your own. **Reread** page 182 of *Lizzie Bright and the Buckminster Boy* in the **Literature Anthology** and answer the questions below.

What details tell you the story is realistic fiction? _____

_____

_____

_____

From whose point of view is this story told? How do you know? _____

_____

_____

_____

_____

Readers to Writers

An engaging plot has an introduction of the conflict, rising action, a climax, falling action, and a resolution. The **introduction** is where the conflict, or problem, is introduced. **Rising action** is what happens as the problem builds. **Climax** is when the problem is confronted. It is the turning point of the story. **Falling action** is what happens right after the climax. **Resolution** is when the problem or conflict is solved.

Plan: Choose Your Topic

Freewrite Think about real experiences that can change a person in some way, such as helping a friend or volunteering for an important cause. What lessons do people learn from these experiences? On a sheet of paper, quickly write your ideas without stopping. Then discuss your ideas with a partner.

Writing Prompt Choose an idea from your freewriting. Write a realistic fiction story in which the main character is changed by something he or she learns from an experience.

I will write my story about _____

_____.

The main character will be _____.

Purpose and Audience Think about who will read or hear your story. Is your purpose to inform, persuade, or entertain? What type of language will you use?

My audience will be _____.

My purpose for writing is to _____.

I will use _____ language to write my story.

 Plan In your writer's notebook, make a chart to plan your story's event sequence. Fill in the first plot event.

> **Quick Tip**
>
> The plot of a story usually has a problem the main character or characters must solve. Write a sentence saying what the main problem is in your story. Then jot down some ideas about how the problem might be solved. Keep this information in mind as you continue to fill in your chart.

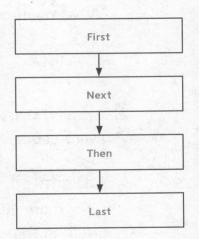

First

↓

Next

↓

Then

↓

Last

Plan: Point of View

Choose Your Narrator Whose perspective, or point of view, do you want to use to tell your story? In first-person point of view (POV), a character tells the story from his or her own perspective. Or would you rather the narrator not be a character in the story? In third-person limited POV, the narrator tells the story from the perspective of one character. A third-person omniscient narrator knows what everyone is thinking. To choose a narrator, ask yourself these questions:

- How much information does the narrator need to know?

- How important is it that the character who experienced the event actually describes it?

- Do readers need to know everyone's thoughts, or just those of one character?

What point of view did you choose and why did you choose it?

_____

_____

 Graphic Organizer Once you have identified your narrator, complete your Event Sequence chart with the main plot events of your story.

Digital Tools

For more information on how to plan events in your realistic fiction story, watch "How to Create a Story Map." Go to **my.mheducation.com**.

Draft

Develop Characters Well-developed characters draw readers into a story. Including descriptive details and dialogue that tell what the characters do, say, and think keeps readers interested. In the example below from "Facing the Storm," notice how the use of descriptive details and dialogue makes Amy and Isabel seem like real people.

> Suddenly, the quiet was shattered by Amy Jensen bursting in and letting the door slam. Isabel felt herself shrink. Amy, who had been a volunteer a bit longer than Isabel, was 16 and strutted around like she owned the place. "Hey, Isabel, I've got a job for you," she barked, planting a hand on Isabel's shoulder.

Now use the excerpt as a model to write a paragraph that could be a part of your realistic fiction story. Use dialogue and descriptive details to bring your characters to life.

_____

_____

_____

_____

 Write a Draft Use your Event Sequence chart to help you write your draft in your writer's notebook. Think about your narrator's point of view as you write. Check that your setting and plot events are realistic. Make sure the ending resolves the story's conflict in a satisfying way.

Quick Tip

To help you develop your characters, write five things about each major character. For example, what do they want the most? What are they afraid of? What is a strength? What is a weakness? Think about how this information fits into your story. Remember, we learn about characters not only through their thoughts and words, but also through their actions.

Revise

Word Choice The use of strong, vivid language in a story helps to create a specific mood. Mood is the feeling the reader gets from a story. Read the paragraph below. Then revise the sentences by using vivid verbs, adjectives, and adverbs that more strongly create a tense mood and sense of urgency.

> Jared struggled in the water. Immediately, I jumped in and started swimming toward him with a life preserver. When I got to Jared, I put the life preserver on him. "It's okay, buddy," I said. He still looked afraid, but began to breathe normally.

_____

_____

_____

_____

_____

_____

 Revision Revise your draft, focusing on vivid verbs and other descriptive language that supports the story's mood. Make sure your story reveals how an experience changes your main character.

Peer Conferences

COLLABORATE

Review a Draft Listen carefully as a partner reads his or her work aloud. Take notes about what you liked and what was difficult to follow. Begin by telling what you liked about the draft. Ask questions that will help the writer think more about the writing. Make suggestions that you think will make the writing stronger. Use these sentence starters.

I liked the way you . . .

This character could be more interesting if . . .

Some vivid verbs here might help . . .

This part is unclear to me. Can you explain why . . .

Partner Feedback After your partner gives you feedback on your draft, write one of the suggestions that you will use in your revision. Refer to the rubric on page 31 as you give feedback.

Based on my partner's feedback, I will _____

_____

_____

_____

After you finish giving each other feedback, reflect on the peer conference. What was helpful? What might you do differently next time?

Revision As you revise your draft, use the Revising Checklist to help you figure out what text you may need to move, elaborate on, or delete. Remember to use the rubric on page 31 to help you with your revision.

✓ Revising Checklist

- ☐ Does my writing fit my purpose and audience?
- ☐ Have I chosen an effective narrator and point of view?
- ☐ Are my characters well developed? Do they talk and act like real people?
- ☐ Do my words support the mood I want to establish? Do I need to add, delete, or rearrange any words?
- ☐ Is my plot realistic? Is there a conflict and a resolution?

Edit and Proofread

When you **edit** and **proofread** your writing, you look for and correct mistakes in spelling, punctuation, capitalization, and grammar. Reading through a revised draft multiple times can help you make sure you're correcting any errors. Use the checklist below to edit your sentences.

✓ Editing Checklist

- ☐ Is dialogue correctly punctuated with quotation marks?
- ☐ Have I used commas correctly, especially in dialogue?
- ☐ Are there any run-on sentences to correct?
- ☐ Are action words used in the proper tense?
- ☐ Are all proper nouns capitalized?
- ☐ Are all words spelled correctly?

Grammar Connections

Sentence fragments are acceptable in realistic fiction dialogue since people often speak in incomplete sentences.

Remember to enclose all dialogue in quotation marks. Set a comma inside the closing quotation mark unless the dialogue is a question or exclamation. For example:

"What time?" Elias asked.

"Around three," Jen answered.

"Great!" Elias said.

List two mistakes you found as you proofread your story.

1 _____

_____

2 _____

_____

Publish, Present, and Evaluate

Publishing When you **publish** your writing, you create a clean, neat final copy that is free of mistakes. If you use cursive writing, make sure to space words correctly.

Presentation When you are ready to **present** your work, rehearse your presentation. Use the Presenting Checklist to help you.

Evaluate After you publish your writing, use the rubric below to **evaluate** your writing.

What did you do successfully? _____

What needs more work? _____

_____

4	3	2	1
• has well-developed characters who act and speak like real people • reflects a clear point of view • has a plot that is engaging and could happen in real life	• has characters who are somewhat developed and mostly act and speak like real people • reflects a point of view that isn't always clear • has a plot that is mostly engaging and could happen in real life	• has characters who are not well-developed and do not often act and speak like real people • reflects a point of view that is often confusing • has a plot that is sometimes engaging and has mostly realistic elements	• has characters who are not well-developed and do not act or speak like real people • is not clear who is telling the story or what point of view is being used • has little plot and could not happen in real life

Talk About It

Helping to build homes for people who can't afford them on their own is a time-honored tradition. Working together with other volunteers increases morale and productivity. Relying on each other's ingenuity helps solve problems and gets the job done right.

Look at the photograph. Talk to a partner about what you see. Discuss what might come out of working together for the common good. Fill in the chart with examples.

SOCIAL STUDIES

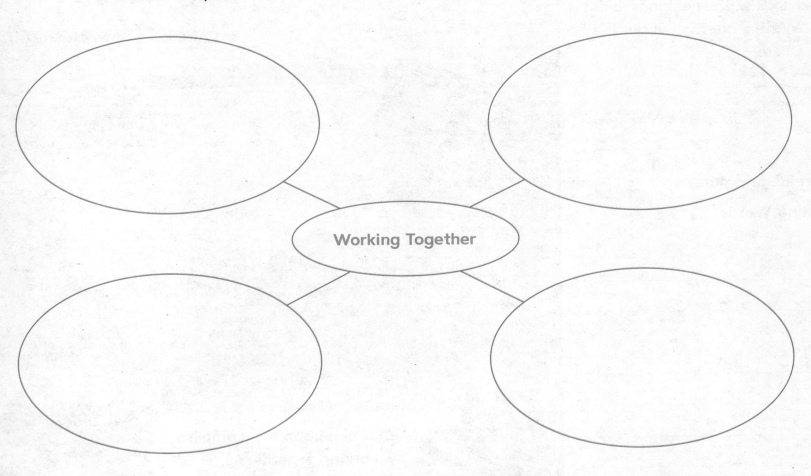

Working Together

BLAST BACK! studysync

Go online to **my.mheducation.com** and read the "For the Good of the Group" Blast. Think about a time when you've heard about someone helping another person. Why might a person help another individual who is in need of help? Then blast back your response.

Justin Sullivan/Getty Images News/Getty Images

TAKE NOTES

Asking questions about a text and then looking for answers helps you set a purpose for reading. Before you read, look at the headings and images. Write a question about the selection here.

_____

_____

_____

As you read, take note of

Interesting Words _____

_____

_____

_____

_____

_____

Key Details _____

_____

_____

_____

_____

_____

_____

Jewels from the Sea

Gideon Mendel/Corbis Documentary/Getty Images

Essential Question

? **What can people accomplish by working together?**

Read about the way one group of women improved their lives and their community.

A Life by the Sea

On their **windswept** island off the coast of eastern Africa, the women of Zanzibar were living much as their ancestors had. They cared for their children and cultivated their gardens. They farmed seaweed from the ocean and gathered shells to sell to tourists who visited their beautiful homeland. Some of the women worked long hours breaking rocks into gravel. Life on the Fumba Peninsula had often been hard for them. They made very little money, and some would say the women were **impoverished**. But they had always managed to feed their families. The ocean had provided for them, supplying **abundant** fish and oysters for food, and colorful shells to sell.

The lustrous interior of an oyster shell

However, gifts from the ocean were not limitless. In the early 2000s, the women began to notice that oysters were not as plentiful as they once had been. In fact, Zanzibar's oysters were being harvested faster than they could replenish themselves. In ten short years, the number of oysters had declined dramatically. The women worried about the uncertain future.

A Fresh Approach

The women began to look beyond the **solitude** of their isolated coastal villages for help. To start, they welcomed the interest of scientists who were studying marine life in the waters surrounding Zanzibar. With guidance from the scientists, the women would work together to manage the way oysters were harvested. They soon discovered they had the power to bring oyster populations back to healthy levels.

Cindy Miller Hopkins/DanitaDelimont.com/Newscom

FIND TEXT EVIDENCE

Read

Paragraphs 1–2
Summarize
Underline details that indicate the women's problem. Then summarize the problem.

_____

_____

Prefixes and Suffixes

How does the prefix *un-*, meaning "not" or "opposite of," help you define *uncertain*?

_____

_____

Paragraph 3
Sequence
Circle the first step the women took to solve their problem.

Reread
Author's Craft

How does the author help you understand the women's problem?

FIND TEXT EVIDENCE 🔍

Read ▾

Paragraph 1

Sequence

What did learning how to make jewelry from oyster shells lead to for the women? **Underline** text that supports your answer.

_____

_____

Paragraphs 2–3

Summarize

Draw a box around the text that explains how mabe pearls form. Summarize the process.

_____

_____

_____

Reread ▾

Author's Craft

Why do you think the author doesn't identify the individual achievements of any one woman?

The women's search for solutions also **unearthed** another new idea. The women had always discarded the oysters' shells after removing the flesh. But visiting experts, who help communities sustain their resources, pointed out that the shells could be valuable, too. They offered to teach the women the skills needed for polishing the shells and turning them into jewelry. Before long, local residents and tourists were buying earrings, necklaces, and bracelets that the women made from shells. The income the women earned from selling jewelry was more than they had ever made before. It occurred to them that, with a little **ingenuity,** they had actually become businesswomen.

Building on Their Success

The women believed they could do even more. They wanted to have control of their business, not to be like a **sharecropper** who owns no land and so keeps only a part of the harvest. It was suggested that they join forces to cultivate *mabe* (MAH-bay) pearls, also known as "half-pearls." These pearls are created when a bead or other irritant is placed inside a living oyster. The oyster coats the irritation with layers of a shiny substance called *nacre* (NAY-ker). The nacre later hardens into a shimmering pearl, perfectly suited for jewelry.

This new project would also work well with the plans to restore the oyster beds. Four "no-take" zones were soon established for the oysters that would produce mabe pearls. There was only one problem. The pearls had to be cultivated underwater. Even though the women had lived all their lives by the sea, they did not know how to swim!

The women are harvesting oysters.

Andrew McConnell/Robert Harding World Imagery/Getty Images

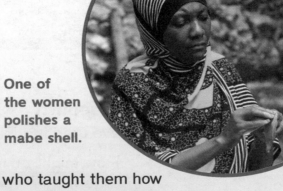

One of the women polishes a mabe shell.

The next step for these strong-willed women was to learn to swim. Others in the village were impressed by the women's determination. Many joined them to help see the project through. The first harvest of mabe pearls in 2008 was so successful that professional jewelers quickly bought up the gleaming harvest to make expensive jewelry.

Toward New Horizons

The women wanted to learn still more ways to improve their business. To do so, they would have to travel thousands of miles across the ocean. Just as learning to swim had been a first, leaving Zanzibar would be a new experience. But together they would go. In 2009, a small group flew to Newport, Rhode Island, in the U.S. to learn about designing and marketing jewelry. They met a master jeweler, who taught them how to wrap strands of fine silver wire into delicate designs around the mabe pearls. They also met people who shared tips on expanding small businesses into large ones. The women absorbed all this and brought it home with them.

The women of Zanzibar still live on their beautiful island. But today there is a difference. By working together, the women have become powerful caretakers of local natural resources and created prosperity in their community. Their hard-earned **productivity** will continue when they teach the next generation of young women how to accomplish great things.

Klaus Hartung

Summarize

Use your notes to orally summarize the most important events in the text. Be sure to summarize them in the order in which they happened.

NARRATIVE NONFICTION

FIND TEXT EVIDENCE 🔍

Read

Paragraph 1
Prefixes and Suffixes
Define *successful* using the suffix *-ful*, meaning "full of" or "having."

_____

_____

Paragraphs 2-3
Voice and Tone
Circle words and phrases that describe the women. How does the author feel about the women?

_____

Synthesize Information
How might restoring oyster populations affect the women's jewelry business?

_____

Reread

Author's Craft

Why is "Toward New Horizons" a good heading for this section?

Vocabulary

Use the example sentences to talk with a partner about each word. Then answer the questions.

abundant

Trees are **abundant** in the forest.

What is abundant in the ocean?

_____

_____

impoverished

In **impoverished** countries, people may not have enough to eat.

What is another word for *impoverished*?

_____

_____

ingenuity

We used **ingenuity** to solve the problem.

How might an inventor show ingenuity?

_____

_____

productivity

Because **productivity** was high, the company had many cars to sell.

What happens when productivity is low?

_____

_____

sharecropper

A **sharecropper** often gives half of what he or she grows to the owner of the land.

Why is it important that a sharecropper have a good crop?

_____

_____

Build Your Word List Reread "A Fresh Approach" on page 35. Circle the word *manage*. In your writer's notebook, use a word web to write more forms of the word. For example, write *management*. Use an online or print dictionary to find more related words. Identify their meanings and use each word in a sentence.

solitude

Josie found a quiet, empty spot to read her book in **solitude**.

What other activities are good to do in solitude?

_____

_____

_____

unearthed

The dog **unearthed** a bone it had buried.

What is an antonym of *unearthed*?

_____

_____

_____

windswept

Sand blew across the **windswept** desert.

Describe what you might see in a windswept field.

_____

_____

_____

Prefixes and Suffixes

Knowing the meanings of prefixes and suffixes can help you define unknown words. Common prefixes include *re-* ("back," "again") and *un-* ("not," "opposite of"). Common suffixes include *-ity* ("quality or state of") and *-ful* ("full of," "having"). Prefixes and suffixes often come from ancient Greek or Latin.

FIND TEXT EVIDENCE

I'm not sure what the meaning of prosperity *is on page 37. I know the Latin suffix* -ity *means "quality or state of." So,* prosperity *must mean "the quality or state of prospering, or living well."*

By working together, the women have become powerful caretakers of local natural resources and created prosperity in their community.

Your Turn Use the prefixes and suffixes above to figure out the meanings of these words from "Jewels from the Sea."

plentiful, *page 35* _____

replenish, *page 35* _____

Summarize

Summarizing a nonfiction narrative text helps you monitor your comprehension and remember what you have learned. Pause after reading each section to identify the main idea for each set of related details. If you are having trouble summarizing the content, reread the text.

 FIND TEXT EVIDENCE

You may not be sure how to summarize the section "A Life by the Sea" on page 35 of "Jewels from the Sea." Reread the section to decide what the important details have in common.

Page 35

> However, gifts from the ocean were not limitless. In the early 2000s, the women began to notice that oysters were not as plentiful as they once had been. In fact, Zanzibar's oysters were being harvested faster than they could replenish themselves. In ten short years, the number of oysters had declined dramatically. The women worried about the uncertain future.

I read details about what the women had done for many years and about how "the number of oysters had declined." I can summarize by saying oysters were being over-harvested. The declining amount of oysters worried the women who depended on them.

Your Turn Reread "Toward New Horizons" on page 37. Summarize how the women of Zanzibar have continued to improve their business.

_____

_____

_____

Quick Tip

Remember that a summary retells just the main ideas and most important details. When a text has headings and subheadings, you can often use them to help you quickly focus on the main idea of a section.

Voice and Tone

Narrative nonfiction such as "Jewels from the Sea" provides factual information in narrative form. This gives an author the chance to express personality, or voice, in a text. One component of voice is tone, or the author's attitude toward a subject. To identify tone, pay attention to the words the author uses to describe the subject of the text. Identifying tone can help you better understand the author's point of view.

🔍 FIND TEXT EVIDENCE

"Jewels from the Sea" explains how a group of women in Zanzibar worked together to improve the economic well-being of their community. The author's tone is kind, respectful, and understanding.

Page 35

A Life by the Sea

On their **windswept** island off the coast of eastern Africa, the women of Zanzibar were living much as their ancestors had. They cared for their children and cultivated their gardens. They farmed seaweed from the ocean and gathered shells to sell to tourists who visited their beautiful homeland. Some of the women worked long hours breaking rocks into gravel. Life on the Fumba Peninsula had often been hard for them. They made very little money, and some would say the women were **impoverished**. But they had always managed to feed their families. The ocean had provided for them, supplying **abundant** fish and oysters for food, and colorful shells to sell.

The lustrous interior of an oyster shell

However, gifts from the ocean were not limitless. In the early 2000s, the women began to notice that oysters were not as plentiful as they once had been. In fact, Zanzibar's oysters were being harvested faster than they could replenish themselves. In ten short years, the number of oysters had declined dramatically. The women worried about the uncertain future.

A Fresh Approach

The women began to look beyond the **solitude** of their isolated coastal villages for help. To start, they welcomed the interest of scientists who were studying marine life in the waters surrounding Zanzibar. With guidance from the scientists, the women would work together to manage the way oysters were harvested. They soon discovered they had the power to bring oyster populations back to healthy levels.

Voice and Tone

The author's voice and tone show how he or she feels about the topic. The tone may be expressed in headings as well as the main text.

Your Turn Read the second paragraph on page 35. Use text evidence to describe the author's tone and point of view.

_____

_____

_____

_____

Sequence

In a nonfiction narrative, the author may organize the text by explaining a sequence of actions or events that occur over time. Identifying each action or event in sequence can help you understand how the outcome came to pass and what the author's message is.

 FIND TEXT EVIDENCE

When I reread the first two sections of "Jewels from the Sea," I can look for actions the women performed to identify and solve their economic problem. As I read on, I can consider all the actions to determine how the women increased their prosperity.

Event
The women realize they have a problem with harvesting oysters.

The women ask for help. They learn how to replenish the oysters and make jewelry from the shells.

> **Quick Tip**
>
> Look for dates and signal words to help you determine the sequence of events. Signal words include words and phrases such as *first, next, eventually, before long,* and *soon after.*

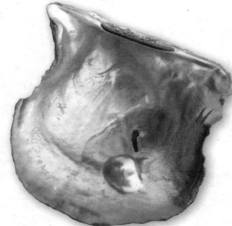

COLLABORATE

Your Turn Reread the rest of "Jewels from the Sea." Identify other key events in the sequence and list them in the graphic organizer.

Event

The women realize they have a problem with harvesting oysters.

↓

The women ask for help. They learn how to replenish the oysters and make jewelry from the shells.

↓

↓

Respond to Reading

COLLABORATE

Discuss the prompt below. Think about how the author conveys information about the women's problem and how they solved it. Use your notes and graphic organizer.

How does the author show what the women of Zanzibar had to do in order to bring prosperity to their community?

_____

_____

_____

_____

_____

_____

_____

_____

_____

_____

_____

_____

_____

Synthesize Information

When you **synthesize** information, you combine several different ideas into one new idea. Synthesizing information from your research on a topic with what you already know allows you to draw conclusions and come to a more complete understanding of your topic.

What information might you synthesize to decide what movie you should see at the theater?

_____

_____

Create a Presentation With a partner or group, create a presentation about a craft associated with a particular culture, ethnic group, or geographic region. Decide what sort of information you would like to include in your presentation. Consider these questions as you research:

- What is the history of the craft?
- Who presently makes the craft? Is it a group effort?
- What materials are used? How is the craft made?

Synthesize what you have learned from your research to create a presentation. What is the best way to share the information on your topic? Do you want to create a slideshow, poster, written report, or something else? Do you want to include audio clips as well as visuals? When you are done, you will share your presentation with the class.

The Gullah culture is known for creating beautiful sweetgrass baskets.

Robert Weller/Shutterstock

The Pot That Juan Built

 How does the author help you understand how Juan was inspired to create his pottery using only local materials?

Literature Anthology: pages 196–207

 Talk About It Reread **Literature Anthology** page 201. Talk about how Juan found his inspiration to create pottery.

Cite Text Evidence What clues help you figure out why Juan uses only local materials? Record your text evidence in the chart.

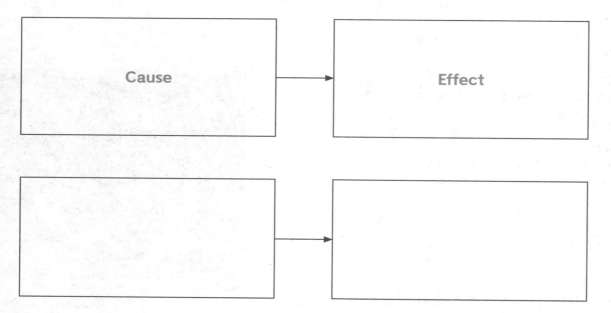

Cause	→	Effect
	→	

Make Inferences

The author mentions that according to Juan's mother, Juan's experiments with minerals and clay left him "always covered in dirt of many colors." What does that tell you about Juan's experiments? How does it give you a sense of his commitment to figuring out how to use local materials in his work?

Write The author helps me understand how Juan was inspired to use local materials by _____

_____

_____

How does the author's use of details help you visualize how Juan gets his materials?

Talk About It Reread **Literature Anthology** page 202. Talk about how Juan collects what he needs to polish his pots.

Cite Text Evidence What words and phrases show the materials Juan uses to polish his clay pots? Write them in the chart and tell what it helps you visualize.

Clues

↓

What I Visualize

Write I can visualize how Juan gets the materials he needs because the author _____

_____

_____

How does the author help you understand how Juan feels about his pottery?

Talk About It Reread **Literature Anthology** page 207. Talk with a partner about Juan's comments about his pottery and how it has affected Mata Ortiz.

Cite Text Evidence What clues help you understand how Juan feels? Record text evidence in the chart below.

Text Evidence	How Juan Feels

Write The author helps me understand how Juan feels about his pottery

by _____

_____

_____

Respond to Reading

COLLABORATE

Discuss the prompt below. Think about what you have learned about the steps Juan follows to create clay pottery. Use your notes and graphic organizer.

How does the author help you understand how local people, plants, animals, and earth are important to Juan's pottery?

_____

_____

_____

_____

_____

_____

_____

_____

_____

_____

_____

_____

_____

Quick Tip

Use these sentence starters to talk about and cite text evidence.

The author describes Juan as . . .

Juan creates pottery using . . .

This is important because he . . .

Self-Selected Reading

Choose a text and fill in your writer's notebook with the title, author, and genre. Record your purpose for reading. For example, you may read to answer a question, or you may read for entertainment.

A Box of Ideas

Literature Anthology:
pages 210–213

Scene 1

Chris *(watching Ms. Cerda)*: What's that box you're making?

Ms. Cerda: It's called a nicho. This one celebrates my mother. First, I made a tin box. Then I punched out a design using a hammer and a tool called an awl, which is like a thick nail, but not so sharp. See how the dots look like a flower? It's a dahlia, my mother's favorite.

Chris: It's Mexico's national flower, too.

Ms. Cerda: That's right, it is.

Inés *(laughing)*: Hey, Chris! Stop pestering my mom.

Gil: I told you he was too young to help out.

Silvia: We could do a car wash.

Inés: No way! My hands are still peeling from the last one.

Reread the excerpt from Scene 1. **Circle** Ms. Cerda's purpose for making her nicho. Then **number** the steps she describes to Chris. Write the numbers beside each step.

COLLABORATE

Talk with a partner about why the author includes directions for how to make a nicho. Where in the excerpt does the author hint at something that will happen later in the play? **Underline** the clues.

Scene 2

Setting: The School Fair, three weeks later

(*Inés, Silvia, Gil, and Chris stand behind a table with a hand-painted sign that says, "Neighborhood Nichos." There is one nicho on the table. Ms. Cerda comes by, picks up the nicho, and looks inside.*)

Ms. Cerda: I'm impressed. You've all become expert nicho makers. This is beautiful.

Inés: I got the shoebox from you, mom!

Silvia: I added the doors – they came from a grocery story carton.

Gil: That one celebrates Main Street. I took pictures of the stores and cars. My uncle printed them out for us.

Chris: I got some wire for the tree trunks from Mr. Marsalis, the electrician next door. The treetops are made of green yarn that Ms. Miller gave us.

Inés: And I added bottle caps to make the car tires.

Ms. Cerda: Very clever. I'm really impressed by your ingenuity.

Reread the excerpt from Scene 2. **Draw a box** around where the author tells you the setting has changed.

Circle how Inés, Silvia, Gil, and Chris all contributed to the neighborhood nicho.

COLLABORATE

Talk with a partner about how Chris got the idea to make nichos. Then use your text markings to discuss how the students got the neighborhood involved. Use text evidence to write your response here:

_____

_____

_____

_____

_____

_____

_____

COLLABORATE

? **Why is "A Box of Ideas" a good title for this selection?**

Talk About It Reread the excerpts on pages 50 and 51. Talk with a partner about what a nicho is and what the conversation between Chris and Ms. Cerda leads to.

Cite Text Evidence What clues help you understand how Ms. Cerda's nicho was the inspiration for the neighborhood nichos? Write evidence in the chart.

Quick Tip

The title of a drama may hint at a theme, or message, that the author wants to share. As you reread "A Box of Ideas," think about what the title means. Then connect that meaning to the events in the drama.

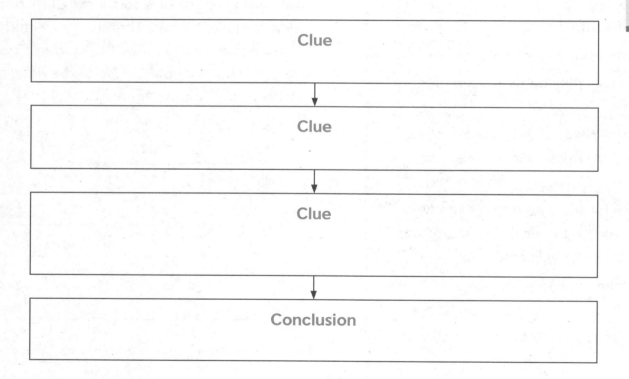

Clue

↓

Clue

↓

Clue

↓

Conclusion

Write "A Box of Ideas" is a good title for this selection because _____

_____

Foreshadowing

Foreshadowing is an author's use of hints or clues about events that will later occur in a story or drama. A character's words, thoughts, and actions can all foreshadow future plot events. Identifying when foreshadowing occurs can help you predict how the plot might unfold.

FIND TEXT EVIDENCE

In the excerpt from Scene 1 of "A Box of Ideas" on page 50, Chris asks Ms. Cerda what she is making. Ms. Cerda tells him about the nicho, a decorative display box. Readers know that the students are trying to think of original ways to raise funds at the School Fair. Chris's interest in Ms. Cerda's nicho hints that he will make one for the fundraiser.

> **Chris** (*watching Ms. Cerda*): What's that box you're making?
>
> **Ms. Cerda:** It's called a nicho. This one celebrates my mother.

Your Turn Reread the excerpts on pages 50 and 51.

- In Scene 1, Gil tells the others that Chris is too young to help out. How does this foreshadow what happens in Scene 2? _____

_____

_____

- How does the author's use of foreshadowing build interest in the story?

_____

_____

Readers to Writers

You can use foreshadowing in your own writing to add interest and suspense. Remember that foreshadowing only hints at events that will occur in a story. Be careful not to give away too much. Foreshadow well before the main event in the story so that readers have time to put the clues together.

Text Connections

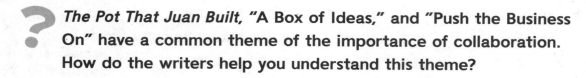

? *The Pot That Juan Built, "A Box of Ideas,"* and *"Push the Business On"* have a common theme of the importance of collaboration. How do the writers help you understand this theme?

COLLABORATE

Talk About It Read the song lyrics. Talk with a partner about what it means to "push the business on." Discuss the theme of the song.

Cite Text Evidence **Circle** the text evidence in the lyrics that describes how the narrators will work to move their goods. **Underline** how they will make the business better.

Write The authors help me understand the theme by

_____

_____

_____

_____

_____

_____

_____

Quick Tip

Repetition helps an author emphasize an idea or message. As you read the lyrics, think about the message the writer is conveying through the repeated phrases, and then compare this idea to the messages the authors convey in the other selections.

Push the Business On

We'll hire a horse and grab a rig;

And all the world will dance a jig;

And we will do whatever we can to push the business on.

To push the business on.

To push the business on.

And we will do whatever we can to push the business on.

Present Your Work

COLLABORATE

Discuss how you will deliver your presentation about a craft associated with a particular culture, ethnic group, or geographic region. Use the Listening Checklist as your classmates give their presentations. Discuss the sentence starters below and write your answers.

One fact I learned while designing my presentation is _____

_____

_____

Now I would like to know more about _____

_____

_____

Quick Tip

Remember to rehearse your presentation beforehand. You may want to have a partner or a group member sit in the back of the room as you practice so you can be sure everyone will be able to clearly hear your voice and see your visuals.

Listening Checklist

☐ Listen actively by taking notes on the presenter's ideas.

☐ Remain attentive so that you can fully understand all the information about the craft presenters are discussing.

☐ Pose relevant questions and ask for clarification or elaboration as needed.

☐ Provide feedback and make pertinent comments.

Essential Question

What steps can people take to promote a healthier environment?

The photograph shows a wind and solar farm, where energy is harvested from the wind and the Sun. Unlike generators that burn fossil fuels, solar farms and wind farms produce electricity without harmful emissions. Advocates for this type of clean, renewable energy say the benefits outweigh any disadvantages.

Look at the photograph. Talk to a partner about what you see. Discuss clean energy sources and their effects. Fill in the web with examples.

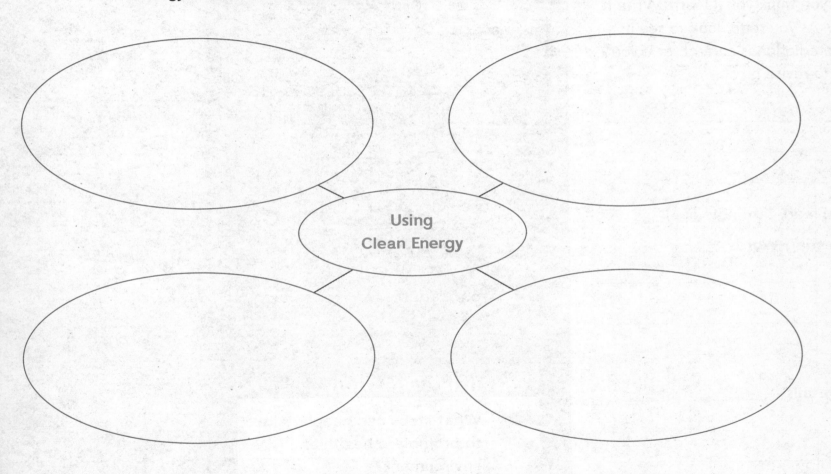

Using
Clean Energy

Go online to **my.mheducation.com** and read the "Tornado Power" Blast. Think about what you know about tornadoes. Why might scientists and engineers want to harness this power, and how might they use it? Blast back your response.

SHARED READ

TAKE NOTES

Before you begin reading, preview the title, headings, and images. Then make a prediction about what you think you'll learn. Write it below. As you read, look to see if your prediction is correct, or if you need to revise it.

_____

_____

_____

As you read, take note of

Interesting Words _____

_____

_____

Key Details _____

_____

_____

_____

_____

Essential Question

?

What steps can people take to promote a healthier environment?

Read about different "green" solutions in the city of the future.

The roof of a barge in London, England, is insulated by several kinds of plants growing on it.

MAKE YOUR CITY GREEN!

These days, people are thankfully trying to be better stewards, or caretakers, of Earth by living in a "green" way. **Advocates** of living in greener communities believe the advantages far outweigh any drawbacks. It is **irrational** to delay solving environmental problems. We can use ideas and technologies available right now to create the city of the future today!

Buildings with Green Roofs

Modern buildings in the green city of the future are designed to save water and energy. Outdated buildings of the past were not. Rooftops covered with grass and other living plants provide **insulation** that keeps buildings cooler. These roofs can also collect, filter, and reuse rainwater that would otherwise be wasted.

Keep It Clean

It is **commonplace** in the green city to use sources of clean energy that are renewable and cause no pollution. Solar panels convert the Sun's energy into electric power. Turbines generate electricity by harvesting the wind's energy on wind farms. Even rivers are harnessed to produce electricity, and geothermal energy from deep within Earth is used to heat homes.

What you won't find in this city are gas stations on every corner. Tax breaks encourage people to use clean energy. And government agencies impose fees on the sale of fossil fuels to discourage their use.

Turbines harvest the wind's energy.

David Wasserman/Brand X Pictures

FIND TEXT EVIDENCE

Read

Paragraphs 1–2
Synonyms and Antonyms
Circle a synonym for *stewards*. What tells you the two words are synonyms?

_____

_____

Write an antonym of the words:

_____

Paragraphs 3–4
Main Idea and Key Details
Underline key details in the section "Keep It Clean." What is the main idea of the section?

_____

_____

Reread

Author's Craft

How do the photographs on these pages help you understand the author's point of view?

FIND TEXT EVIDENCE

Read

Paragraphs 1–2

Ask and Answer Questions

What question can you ask and answer about the information in this section? Write the question. **Underline** the answer.

_____

_____

Paragraphs 3–4

Problem and Solution

Write a problem that the citizens of the green city solve. **Draw a box** around the solution.

_____

_____

Reread

Author's Craft

How does the author convey the importance of composting?

TIME FOR KIDS

Moving Right Along

Most people in the green city of the future **designate** mass transit as their preferred method of travel. Since passengers who have chosen to ride trains are not driving their cars, less fuel is burned. Any private cars still in use are hybrid or plug-in electric vehicles. Hybrid cars run on both fuel and batteries. Some electric cars do not use gas at all. Instead, owners plug their cars into standard electrical outlets to charge the batteries.

In the green city, many cars, trucks, and buses burn fuels made from renewable sources rather than oil. For example, a biofuel called ethanol is made from corn and sugar cane crops. Biodiesel is made from soybean oil, animal fat, or even cooking grease!

Open Spaces

Citizens of the green city understand that protecting native species is key to conserving natural spaces. Because native plants are original to the ecosystem, they provide the **optimal** habitat for local insects, birds, and other animals. Native plants that are well adapted to the local climate also require less water. Imported plants are quickly identified and removed. Otherwise, they may become **invasive** and overwhelm local species.

Residents recognize that a process called *composting* helps reduce the amount of solid waste that is sent to landfills. It also increases the richness of local soil. People mix food scraps and yard waste with water and air in large bins. Helpful bacteria and fungi then break down this pile of "garbage" into an eco-friendly and economical fertilizer that improves the health of city parks and backyards.

(t) Ingram Publishing; (b) Eurasia Press/Photononstop/Getty Images

An electric car is plugged into a recharging station.

HOW TO MAKE COMPOST

Cooking up some rich compost is easy when you follow these steps.

"Green" (Wet) Material (nitrogen-rich)

- grass; garden trimmings
- food scraps: fruits and vegetables (no meat, bones, dairy products, or grease)
- coffee grounds and filters; tea bags
- egg shells

"Brown" (Dry) Material (carbon-rich)

- autumn leaves
- straw
- sawdust
- shredded newspapers

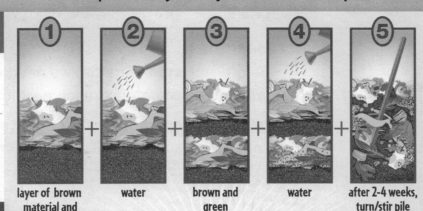

① + ② + ③ + ④ + ⑤

layer of brown material and layer of green material + water + brown and green + water + after 2-4 weeks, turn/stir pile

Karen Minot

COMPOST

repeat steps 1 through 5 for 2 more months

Your House Should Be More Passive!

POINT COUNTERPOINT

I believe that all new houses should be "passive" homes. This means they would be built with materials and systems that reduce energy use. Most people think it's too expensive to do this. Actually, the savings over several years on the cost of electricity and carbon-based heating fuels soon exceed the higher **initial** cost of the energy-saving features. Some families are concerned that "thermal mass" floors used to retain heat in winter are too unattractive. Or they may think that keeping plants alive on the roof is too difficult. But these objections don't take into account a growing number of flooring styles and easy-to-maintain "green" roofing systems. The combined benefits of lower energy costs and less pollution from fossil fuels are reason enough to build more passive homes.

Summarize

Summarize "Make Your City Green!" to a partner. Discuss the prediction you made on page 58. Was it correct? Why?

FIND TEXT EVIDENCE

Read

Flowchart
Ask and Answer Questions

What question can the flowchart help you answer? Write the question and **circle** the answer.

_____

_____

Sidebar
Main Idea and Key Details

Draw a box around the main idea. **Underline** supporting key details.

Reread

Author's Craft

What is the author's purpose for including the sidebar "Your House Should Be More Passive!"?

Fluency

Read the sidebar to a partner. Discuss what helps you read accurately at an appropriate rate.

Vocabulary

Use the example sentences to talk with a partner about each word. Then answer the questions.

advocates

Advocates for open space fight to improve local and national parks.

What is one cause advocates have worked for in your community?

_____

_____

commonplace

In some areas, it is **commonplace** for kids to play kickball during their free time.

What is a commonplace homework assignment that you receive?

_____

_____

designate

Before starting the game, we need to **designate** which teammate plays each position.

What happens when you designate money for something, such as a class trip?

_____

_____

initial

Lin changed her answer after she realized that her **initial** response was incorrect.

What is an antonym of *initial*?

_____

_____

insulation

A bird's inner feathers provide natural **insulation**.

Where is insulation used in a building?

_____

_____

Build Your Word List Pick a word you found interesting in the selection you read. Look up synonyms and antonyms of the word in a thesaurus and write them in your writer's notebook.

invasive

That plant is **invasive** and will take over the garden if it's not removed.

When might noise feel invasive?

_____

_____

_____

irrational

Even though I know most spiders are harmless, I have an **irrational** fear of all spiders.

What is a synonym for _irrational?_

_____

_____

_____

optimal

Often, the **optimal** time for fishing is early in the morning.

What are optimal conditions for playing outdoor sports?

_____

_____

_____

Synonyms and Antonyms

Synonyms are words with the same or similar meanings. **Antonyms** have opposite meanings. You can use the relationship between synonyms and antonyms in the same sentence or paragraph as clues to help you find the meaning of one or both words.

FIND TEXT EVIDENCE

On page 59 of "Make Your City Green!" the text says that "advantages far outweigh any drawbacks." The advantages are being contrasted to the drawbacks. This makes me think the words have opposite meanings. Drawbacks must be an antonym of advantages.

Advocates of living in greener communities believe the advantages far outweigh any drawbacks.

Your Turn Find a nearby synonym or antonym for each word from "Make Your City Green!" Explain how you identified the synonym or antonym.

modern, _page 59_ _____

_____

imported, _page 60_ _____

David Wasserman/Brand X Pictures

Ask and Answer Questions

When you reread an argumentative text, you can pause to ask yourself questions about sections that were unclear to you the first time you read them. Looking in the text for the answers to your questions can help you understand the information.

 **FIND TEXT EVIDENCE**

When you first read the section "Buildings with Green Roofs" on page 59, it may not have been clear to you why buildings should have green roofs.

Page 59

Buildings with Green Roofs

Modern buildings in the green city of the future are designed to save water and energy. Outdated buildings of the past were not. Rooftops covered with grass and other living plants provide **insulation** that keeps buildings cooler. These roofs can also collect, filter, and reuse rainwater that would otherwise be wasted.

I asked myself why people would want a green roof. I read that a green roof saves water and energy by keeping buildings cooler and reusing rainwater. I can infer from this that green roofs save money and protect the environment.

Your Turn What does the author mean by "clean energy"? Reread the section "Keep It Clean" on page 59. Tell how you used details from the section to answer the question.

_____

_____

_____

Problem and Solution

"Make Your City Green!" is an argumentative text. An argumentative text provides reasons and factual evidence to support an author's claim. It may include a problem-and-solution text structure to argue for certain solutions to a problem. Graphic and text features, such as flowcharts and sidebars, may also help support the author's claim.

 FIND TEXT EVIDENCE

"Make Your City Green!" discusses the need for a "green" environment and the ways people are filling this need. The flowchart and sidebar provide more information about two possible solutions.

Readers to Writers

To determine an appropriate text structure to use in your writing, consider the kind of writing you are doing. Problem-and-solution text structure can be a good way to organize argumentative text. It requires you to address a problem or challenge and suggest what might be done about it.

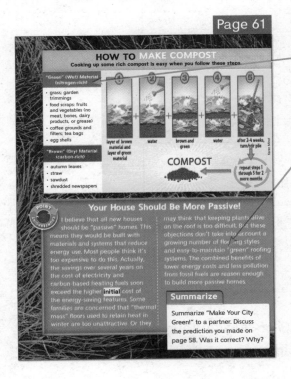

Page 61

Flowcharts

Flowcharts show the steps in a process.

Sidebars

A sidebar can be used to give additional arguments in support of a claim. It can support claims by presenting specific solutions to problems raised by opposing opinions.

Your Turn Explain how each text feature on page 61 helps the author present a solution to a problem.

COLLABORATE

Main Idea and Key Details

The main, or central, idea is the overall point the author makes about a topic, but it may not be stated directly. If no sentence in the text states the idea that ties all the key details together, use what the details have in common to identify the main idea.

 FIND TEXT EVIDENCE

When I reread the section "Moving Right Along" on page 60, I can think about how the key details are connected to help me identify the main idea.

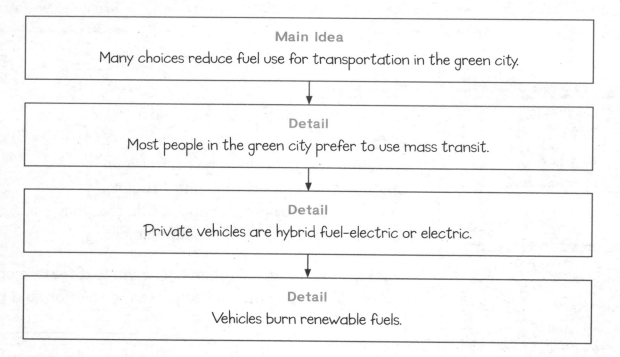

Main Idea
Many choices reduce fuel use for transportation in the green city.

⬇

Detail
Most people in the green city prefer to use mass transit.

⬇

Detail
Private vehicles are hybrid fuel-electric or electric.

⬇

Detail
Vehicles burn renewable fuels.

COLLABORATE

Your Turn Reread the section "Open Spaces" on page 60 of "Make Your City Green!" Identify key details and use what they have in common to determine the main idea of the section.

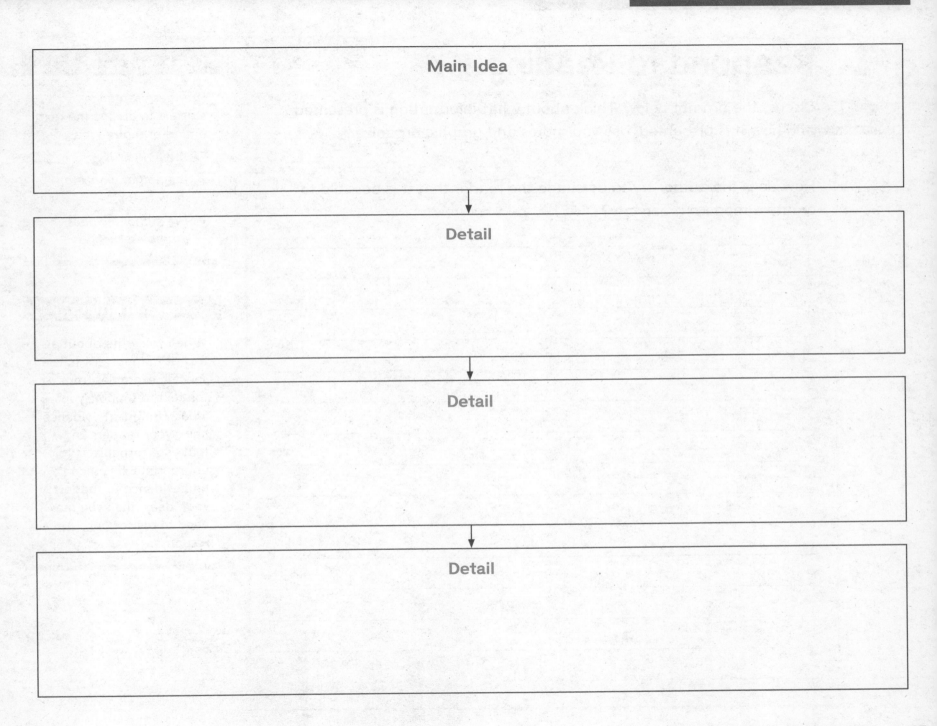

Main Idea

↓

Detail

↓

Detail

↓

Detail

Respond to Reading

COLLABORATE

Discuss the prompt below. Think about what information is presented and how it is presented. Use your notes and graphic organizer.

How does the author try to persuade the reader that it is possible to create a modern green city?

_____

_____

_____

_____

_____

_____

_____

_____

_____

_____

_____

_____

_____

Develop a Plan

In a debate, two sides present opposing arguments about a specific issue or idea. Debates have formats that must be followed. A moderator keeps track of time, keeps the debaters on topic, and reminds them to observe the rules.

What do you think is one important rule for a debate? Write it here:

_____

Debate In groups of six, divide into two teams to plan a debate about which mode of travel is better: mass transit or cars. Each team will take opposing views. Look at the debate format and decide who will be the speaker for each part of the debate. As you research and prepare your debate, make sure you have

- an introduction clearly stating your side's position;
- reasons and factual evidence to support your claim;
- an understanding of the opposing view so you can refute it;
- a conclusion that restates the most important points.

Once you've prepared your material, the two sides within your group will present their positions in a debate for the class.

Debate Format

- A speaker from each team presents an argument that supports a position.

- A speaker from each team gives a rebuttal, refuting the opposing team's positions.

- A speaker from each team responds to the rebuttal, summarizes the team's position, and closes with reasons the team's position is preferable.

Stewards of the Environment

? **Why does the author begin the selection with information about President Theodore Roosevelt?**

Literature Anthology: pages 214–217

Talk About It Reread the first two paragraphs on **Literature Anthology** page 215. Talk with a partner about President Roosevelt's conservation efforts.

Cite Text Evidence How does the author transition from the work Roosevelt did to what conservationists are doing today? Record text evidence in the chart and tell how the transition is made.

Text Evidence	How the Transition is Made

Synthesize Information

Consider what you know about ways in which both the U.S. government and individuals have promoted conservation efforts since Roosevelt's time. What does this tell you about Roosevelt and his ideas about conservation and protecting the environment?

Write The author begins the selection with information about President

Roosevelt to _____

_____

How does the author use text features to help you understand the importance of recycling?

 Talk About It Reread **Literature Anthology** page 217. Talk with a partner about what it takes to start a recycling program.

Cite Text Evidence How does the organization of the information help you understand it better? Use this chart to record text evidence. Describe what each text feature shows. Then say how it helps you understand recycling.

Flowchart	Photograph and Caption	How It Helps

Write The author uses text features to help me _____

_____

_____

_____

Respond to Reading

COLLABORATE

Discuss the prompt below. Think about what you know about how an author conveys, or shows, his or her feelings about a topic. Use your notes and graphic organizer.

How does the author feel about people who work to address environmental problems?

_____

_____

_____

_____

_____

_____

_____

_____

_____

_____

_____

_____

_____

Quick Tip

Use these sentence starters to talk about and cite text evidence.

The author feels that . . .

The author shares an opinion by . . .

This helps me understand . . .

Self-Selected Reading

Choose a text to read independently. Read the first two pages. If five or more words are unfamiliar, you may decide to pick another text. Fill in your writer's notebook with the title, author, and genre of the book. Include a personal response to the text in your writer's notebook.

Modern Transit for an Ancient City

Literature Anthology:
pages 218–219

1   In September 1997, the city of Athens, Greece, won the honor of hosting the 2004 summer Olympic Games. A key factor in the decision was the city's promise to have a modern metro (subway) system ready to serve people who came to the games. Most people who live in cities around the world are advocates of mass transit. Busses and trains move large numbers of people while minimizing the use of fossil fuels. Even a city as ancient as Athens can and should have a "green" mass transit system, Olympics or no Olympics.

2   Greece has a population of over 10.5 million people. Nearly half of them are crowded into the city of Athens. Before 1994, polluting emissions from cars and other vehicles were completely unregulated. Athens was frequently shrouded in smog. The dirty air was unhealthy for people, and it was damaging the ancient cultural treasures of Greece, including the Parthenon and other monuments.

Underline the sentence in paragraph 1 that states the author's argument. **Circle** words and phrases in paragraph 2 that describe Athens before mass transit.

COLLABORATE

Talk with a partner about how the author feels about mass transit. Use text evidence to support your response. Write it here:

_____

_____

_____

_____

_____

_____

_____

_____

_____

How does the author use descriptive language to help you visualize mass transit and understand his or her perspective?

COLLABORATE

Talk About It Reread the excerpt on page 73. Talk with a partner about how the author describes mass transit.

Cite Text Evidence What clues help you understand the author's perspective on mass transit? Record text evidence in the chart.

Clues	→	Author's Perspective

Quick Tip

An author's choice of words and phrases can reveal a lot about his or her perspective. As you read, think about the words the author uses to tell about something. Then think about whether the words give a positive or negative feeling.

Write The author reveals a perspective on mass transit by _____

_____

_____

Evaluate Claims

A **claim** is an author's position or perspective on an idea or issue. Credible, or believable, claims are supported by factual reasons and evidence. Authors may further strengthen the credibility of claims by addressing and refuting opposing arguments.

🔍 FIND TEXT EVIDENCE

On page 73, the author of "Modern Transit for an Ancient City" provides a reason to support his or her claim that cities should have green transportation systems. The author says that doing so would transport many people and reduce fossil fuel use.

> Busses and trains move large numbers of people while minimizing the use of fossil fuels. Even a city as ancient as Athens can and should have a "green" mass transit system, Olympics or no Olympics.

Your Turn Reread paragraphs 3 and 4 on **Literature Anthology** page 219.

- How does the author address an opposing argument? _____

_____

_____

- Is the author's claim credible? Explain your reasoning. _____

_____

_____

Quick Tip

When you address and refute an opposing argument, you first tell what that argument is. Then you refute it, or prove it wrong.

Readers to Writers

Check that your reasons and evidence are objective. Objective support for a claim is factual information and not opinion. Providing objective support makes it more likely that readers will evaluate your claim as valid, or credible.

Text Connections

? **How does the way the photographer frames Lingang New City compare with the way the authors organize text in *Stewards of the Environment* and "Modern Transit for an Ancient City"?**

Talk About It Look at the photograph and read the caption. Talk with a partner about what you see. Discuss why the photographer used this angle to photograph Lingang New City.

Cite Text Evidence **Circle** clues in the photograph that help you see what the photographer thinks is important. **Underline** evidence in the caption that supports what the photographer wants you to know.

Write The photographer and authors organize their information to help me

_____

_____

_____

_____

_____

George Hammerstein/Corbis/Glow Images

Quick Tip

Think about other framing options that might have been available to the photographer. Consider how these options might affect a viewer's ability to understand why Lingang New City is considered a "green city." Tell your ideas to your partner.

This residential area in Lingang New City, China, features rows of apartment buildings with rooftop solar panels. Lingang New City is a trial "green city" that relies on solar power for all its energy and will feature energy-saving technology and only electric cars and ferries.

Accuracy and Rate

Reading argumentative text with **accuracy** means pronouncing words correctly. As you read, look for challenging vocabulary that might require careful pronunciation. You may need to adjust your **rate**, or speed. Read more slowly so the words are clear and correct.

Page 60

> People mix food scraps and yard waste with water and air in large bins. Helpful bacteria and fungi then break down this pile of "garbage" into an eco-friendly and economical fertilizer that improves the health of city parks and backyards.

Think about how you would use punctuation to adjust your rate.

Think of the correct pronunciation of each syllable of a multisyllabic word.

Quick Tip

Before you read aloud, look at the text. See what kind of text it is so you can plan your rate. You might want to read scientific information more slowly to give yourself time to accurately read difficult words.

Your Turn Turn back to page 59. Take turns reading aloud the section "Keep It Clean" with a partner. Think about how to read scientific terms and words with multiple syllables. Plan your rate of reading so that you can read with accuracy.

Afterward, think about how you did. Complete the sentences below.

I remembered to _____

_____.

Next time I will _____

_____.

Expert Model

Literature Anthology:
pages 218–219

Features of a Persuasive Article

A persuasive article is a form of argumentative text. It presents a viewpoint, or opinion, about a topic and tries to convince the reader of that viewpoint. A persuasive article

- clearly introduces the author's claim about the issue or topic;

- supports the argument with clear reasons and relevant evidence, such as facts, details, statistics, and quotes;

- ends with a strong conclusion that aims to convince the audience to agree with the claim.

Analyze an Expert Model Studying argumentative texts will help you write your own persuasive article. **Reread** page 218 of "Modern Transit for an Ancient City" in the **Literature Anthology**, and then answer the questions below.

What claim does the author present? _____

_____

_____

What evidence does the author use to support the claim? _____

_____

_____

Word Wise

On page 218, the author uses words that reveal his or her opinion about "green" mass transit systems. The word *should* in the last sentence of the first paragraph indicates that this is the author's opinion. Other words and phrases that signal opinion include *clearly, definitely, I feel, I think, I believe, always,* and *never.*

Plan: Choose Your Topic

Mapping With a partner, talk about environmental issues. What positions do people take on the issues? On a separate sheet of paper, create a web to map your ideas.

Writing Choose one environmental issue that you recorded in your web, and then write a persuasive article in which you convince your readers to support your opinion.

I will write about _____.

I will make the claim that _____.

Purpose and Audience Think about who will read or hear your article. What will be your purpose for writing? Then think about language that will help you best convey your purpose.

My purpose for writing is _____.

My audience will be _____.

I will use _____ language to write my persuasive article.

Plan Think about what you want your readers to know about the issue you chose. Write down questions in your writer's notebook and look for the answers as you research the issue. The answers will help you develop reasons for your claim. Your questions might include: *Why is this an important issue? How would solving the problem affect the environment? What might happen if the issue is not eventually resolved?* Take notes on specific facts and details in your answers.

Quick Tip

Examples of environmental topics might include

- using fossil fuels;
- reducing noise pollution;
- harnessing solar energy;
- increasing funding for mass transit.

You can also search online for more ideas about environmental topics.

Plan: Reasons and Evidence

Support a Claim You will need to give reasons for your claim. In order to be convincing, the reasons must be supported by evidence. A reason explains why you are making the claim. Evidence includes facts, statistics, and examples that support your claim. Your evidence should come from reliable sources. As you think about your reasons and gather evidence, ask:

- Why is it important to support this side of the issue?

- How relevant is this piece of evidence? Does it support my claim?

- What evidence will help refute opposing arguments or ideas?

List one reason and two pieces of evidence you could use in your persuasive article.

Reason: _____

_____

Evidence 1: _____

_____

Evidence 2: _____

_____

Quick Tip

Paraphrase the important ideas from your research and check that you have accurately recorded any quotations you plan to use. Keep track of your sources so you can cite them.

Tech Tip

Use technology to help organize your notes and sources. For example, you can set up a simple spreadsheet to enter and sort publication details (title, author, date, URL) for your sources.

Graphic Organizer In your writer's notebook, create an Evidence/ Conclusions organizer to plan your writing. Use your research notes to fill in the Evidence section with examples of strong, relevant evidence. In the Conclusions section, explain how the evidence supports your claim.

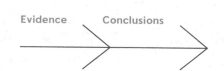

Draft

Strong Conclusion The conclusion of a persuasive article is the author's last chance to convince readers to agree with his or her claim or viewpoint. In the example below from "Trees for a Healthier Africa," the conclusion summarizes and reinforces the author's point of view that we need to reverse deforestation and that there are ways to do to this.

> Reversing deforestation takes time, but many people are working to turn it around. People have chosen not to make the same mistakes again, and by working together they hope to improve the earth's environment.

Now use the paragraph above as a model to draft a conclusion you might use in your persuasive article.

_____

_____

_____

_____

_____

 Write a Draft Use your Evidence/Conclusions graphic organizer to help you write your draft in your writer's notebook. Remember to start your article by clearly introducing your topic and claim.

Quick Tip

• What is the most important thing you want the reader to remember about your argument? Make sure you include that idea in your conclusion.

• Conclusions to persuasive articles also often include "a call to action," or what the writer wants the readers to do about the issue.

Revise

Sentence Structure Focusing on sentence structure can help you make your ideas clearer and more engaging. Combining sentences that repeat information eliminates wordiness. Adding transition words such as *however, similarly, although,* and *therefore* helps readers recognize relationships among claims, reasons, and evidence. Read the passage below. Then revise it by combining sentences and adding transition words.

> Some people object to wind turbines. They say wind turbines are noisy. Some people say wind turbines can be dangerous to local wildlife. Not true. Wind turbines are neither of those things if communities use them thoughtfully. Wind turbines have their flaws. But they still have advantages for the environment.

> **Quick Tip**
>
> Read these sentences: *I think it is a good idea to have hybrid cars. Hybrid cars can run on fuel. They can also run on batteries.* What words and ideas repeat in these sentences? These sentences can be combined by eliminating the repetition: *Hybrid cars are a good idea because they can run on both fuel and batteries.*

_____

_____

_____

_____

 Revise Revise your draft. Check that you have combined sentences and used transition words that clarify the relationships among your claim, reasons, and evidence.

Peer Conferences

COLLABORATE

Review a Draft Listen carefully as a partner reads his or her work aloud. Take notes about what you liked and what was difficult to follow. Begin by telling what you liked about the draft. Ask questions that will help the writer think more about the writing. Make suggestions that you think will make the writing stronger. Use these sentence starters.

I found your claim credible because . . .

This reason could better support your claim if you . . .

Your conclusion was/was not persuasive because . . .

Partner Feedback After your partner gives you feedback on your draft, write one of the suggestions that you will use in your revision. Refer to the rubric on page 85 as you give feedback.

Based on my partner's feedback, I will _____

_____.

After you finish giving each other feedback, reflect on the peer conference. What was helpful? What might you do differently next time?

Revision As you revise your draft, use the Revising Checklist to help you figure out what text you may need to move, elaborate on, or delete. Remember to use the rubric on page 85 to help you with your revision.

Digital Tools

For more information about peer conferences, watch "Peer Conferencing (Collaborative Conversations Video)." Go to **my.mheducation.com**.

✔ Revising Checklist

- ☐ Does my writing fit my purpose and audience?
- ☐ Did I introduce the topic and state a clear claim?
- ☐ Do my reasons and evidence provide strong support for the claim?
- ☐ Do I need to combine sentences to delete repeating words or ideas?
- ☐ Do I need to strengthen my conclusion in order to convince readers to agree with my claim?

Edit and Proofread

When you **edit** and **proofread** your writing, you look for and correct mistakes in spelling, punctuation, capitalization, and grammar. Reading through a revised draft multiple times can help you make sure you're correcting any errors. Use the checklist below to edit your sentences.

Grammar Connections

As you proofread, make sure that all verbs, including irregular ones, are used correctly. Irregular verbs are verbs that do not end in *-ed* to form the past tense. For example, the past tense of *bring* is *brought*.

✔ Editing Checklist

☐ Can sentence fragments be combined into a complete thought?

☐ Are all verbs used correctly?

☐ Are any shifts in pronoun number or person present?

☐ Are compound and complex sentences punctuated correctly?

☐ Are commas used correctly?

☐ Are all words spelled correctly?

List two mistakes you found as you proofread your persuasive article.

1 _____

_____

2 _____

_____

Publish, Present, and Evaluate

Publishing When you **publish** your writing, you create a clean, neat final copy that is free of mistakes. As you write, be sure to print neatly and leave spaces between words. Consider adding visuals such as diagrams, maps, or photographs to help make your claim and reasons more persuasive.

Presentation When you are ready to **present** your work, rehearse your presentation. Use the Presenting Checklist to help you.

Evaluate After you publish your writing, use the rubric below to **evaluate** your writing.

What did you do successfully? _____

What needs more work? _____

_____

✓ Presenting Checklist

- ☐ Engage your audience by making eye contact.
- ☐ Speak clearly, slowly, and loudly enough so that everyone can understand you.
- ☐ Respond to the audience's reactions. For example, if people seem confused, slow down the pace.
- ☐ Practice using visuals so that you can refer to them without interrupting your presentation.
- ☐ Address comments or questions respectfully.

4	3	2	1
• states the topic and expresses a clear claim	• states the topic, but the claim is somewhat unclear	• states the topic but lacks a claim	• does not state the topic or a claim
• provides several reasons and relevant evidence based on research	• provides some reasons and relevant evidence based on research	• provides few reasons and evidence based on research; some evidence is unrelated to topic	• provides no reasons or evidence; no obvious research has been done
• ends with a strong conclusion that restates and reinforces the claim	• ends with a conclusion that restates and reinforces the claim	• ends with a conclusion that vaguely refers to the claim and reasons	• lacks a strong conclusion

Spiral Review

You have learned new skills and strategies in Unit 3 that will help you read more critically. Now it is time to practice what you have learned.

- **Problem and Solution**
- **Prefixes/Suffixes**
- **Main Idea and Key Details**
- **Theme**
- **Make Inferences**
- **Context Clues**
- **Point of View**

Connect to Content

- **Create a Sidebar**
- **"Elephant Camp"**

Read the selection and choose the best answer to each question.

The Power of Wind

Charles Brush built this wind turbine at his home in Cleveland, Ohio.

[1] For thousands of years, people have taken advantage of a natural power source: the wind. Since ancient times, wind has helped people sail across great bodies of water. Wind turns windmills that pump water and grind grain.

[2] In 1888, Charles Brush took the power of wind one step further. He built America's first wind turbine, an engine that produces electricity by harnessing the power of the wind. Brush's wind turbine produced a small amount of energy, but modern turbines can produce enough electricity to power thousands of homes. That leads some people to believe that wind power is a great replacement for the fossil fuels that contribute to environmental pollution. Others, however, say there are problems with the technology.

Catch the Wind!

[3] Advocates of wind power build a strong case for its use. They point out that wind is constantly generated, so the supply will never run out. They also argue that if we get more power from a renewable energy source like wind, we can limit our use of fossil fuels for energy. This would cut down on the release of carbon dioxide, methane, and other greenhouse gases into the atmosphere. Scientists tell us these gases contribute to changes in Earth's climate.

4   Cost is another advantage, say proponents. One problem with gas, coal, and other fossil fuels is their unpredictable cost. Prices rise and fall, which poses a challenge to those who rely on these resources for energy. Wind, however, is free. Supporters argue that transitioning to wind power is a way to relieve the financial stress experienced by businesses and communities that rely on fossil fuels.

5   Wind power also offers economic advantages to communities. In some areas, the government offers to reduce property taxes if communities build wind farms on open tracts of land. This can be a financial benefit for people living in those locations. The wind industry also provides jobs for people to build, operate, and maintain turbines. In fact, according to the U.S. Department of Energy, as many as 600,000 people could be employed by the industry by 2050.

This wind farm in California contains thousands of turbines.

Be Gone with the Wind!

6   Not everyone believes in the potential of wind energy, though. Opponents point out that wind is <u>unreliable</u>. What if calm winds fail to produce the amount of energy we require? What if strong winds during a storm damage the turbines?

7   Opponents also claim that the low cost of wind energy is misleading. While wind itself may be free, building just one commercial turbine can cost millions of dollars.

8   Opponents also have environmental concerns. Some people say wind farms are eyesores that ruin the beauty of the natural landscape. In addition, the rotating blades generate noise, which is another kind of pollution. And spinning turbine blades can endanger birds, bats, and other flying wildlife.

The Future

9   Despite these competing opinions, it's likely that the United States will draw a greater proportion of its energy usage from the wind in the coming years. Perhaps groups and individuals on both sides of this issue can work together to ensure the technology improves and is used appropriately.

Kim Steele/Getty Images

SHOW WHAT YOU LEARNED

1 The main idea of paragraph 2 is that —

   A Charles Brush made wind a viable energy source

   B we should be using more wind energy to power our homes

   C modern-day wind energy is controversial

   D wind is an unlimited source of energy

2 In paragraph 3, the reader can infer that —

   F fossil fuels are nonrenewable resources

   G wind power is not very useful

   H gases prevent oxygen from circulating in the atmosphere

   J gases are found in the upper atmosphere

3 In paragraph 4, the author uses a problem and solution structure to —

   A show how some believe wind power to be a cost-effective alternative to fossil fuels

   B describe the challenges of wind power

   C help readers see the benefits of gas, coal, and other fossil fuels

   D communicate how expensive wind power is

4 What is the meaning of <u>unreliable</u> in paragraph 6?

   F not useful

   G not easy

   H not dependable

   J not practical

Quick Tip

Don't spend too much time on any one question. If you get stuck, move on to the next question. You can always go back and answer the more difficult questions later.

Read the selection and choose the best answer to each question.

Elena's Audition

1   Elena awoke in the middle of the night to see lamplight from the street filtering through her window and casting a square of yellow light on her bedroom floor. Her room was still strange and unfamiliar to her, especially in the dark. Elena and her father had moved into their new city apartment from a suburban neighborhood just weeks earlier.

2   Elena looked at the clock with <u>weary</u> eyes. The glowing digital display read two o'clock. Elena groaned. "This is unbearable!" she said, much more loudly than she had intended.

3   Elena's father appeared at her door. "Awake so early?"

4   Elena chewed her lip. "Auditions for the school orchestra are tomorrow," she said. "What if the music teachers don't like my playing? What if the other kids play better than I do?"

5   Elena had not had any trouble clinching a spot in the trumpet section of the orchestra at her old school. But her new school in the city was bigger and had many more students. She feared the competition would be fierce. She knew Mr. and Ms. Johnson, the music teachers at her new school, lived in the same apartment building that she and her father did, but she hadn't met them yet. What if they weren't as friendly as the teachers in her old school?

6   "Elena, you're one of the most talented young trumpet players I've ever heard," her father reassured her. "Your new school's orchestra is going to be lucky to have you. Try to get some rest and trust in your talent. You will do just fine tomorrow."

7   Elena's father turned into the hallway and gently closed her bedroom door. Elena set her head against the pillow and let out a slow sigh. She had been practicing her trumpet playing every day and had learned some very difficult pieces. But the thought of playing in front of many new people was unnerving.

8   Elena closed her eyes and tried to lull herself back to sleep by focusing on the quiet hum of cars passing on the street outside. And then she smelled it—a foul, acrid odor. Something electrical was burning. She grimaced in response to the awful stench.

9   "Dad, a fire!" she yelled. Elena's father burst through the door as she was hoisting herself into her wheelchair. He checked for smoke and flames in the hallway and, seeing it was clear, pushed Elena toward the door. In one swift motion he grabbed Elena's trumpet case that had been resting by the door. They fled their first-floor apartment and traveled a safe distance from the building on the sidewalk outside.

10   Neighbors started to join Elena and her father outside. They watched as thin wisps of smoke began to reach into the sky. Elena's father was calling 911. Smoke alarms sounded faintly from many of the apartment units, but Elena worried for neighbors who might be fast asleep in apartments where the smoke had not yet reached. She also heard distant sirens, but how long would it take for help to arrive?

11   Elena unsnapped the metal clasps on her trumpet case. She lifted her trumpet, its polished brass catching the light from the streetlamps above. With as much power as she could muster, Elena played loud, ear-grabbing notes.

12   More people, including Mr. and Ms. Johnson, emerged from the building. Firemen leapt from bright red trucks that had just arrived. Soon the fire was extinguished.

13   Mr. and Ms. Johnson approached Elena and her father. "We heard your trumpet! Such quick thinking!" said Ms. Johnson. "And what powerful playing!"

14   "I hope you plan on joining our school orchestra!" said Mr. Johnson.

15   Elena smiled as her father put his arm around her. Suddenly she wasn't feeling so nervous.

1 The story's point of view can be described as —

   A first-person, from Elena's point of view

   B third-person, limited to Elena's thoughts and feelings

   C third-person, limited to the thoughts and feelings of Elena's father

   D third-person omniscient

2 The word <u>weary</u> in paragraph 2 means —

   F covered

   G open

   H tired

   J unfocused

3 What can you infer about Elena from details in the story?

   A She is very unhappy with her new school.

   B She doesn't like the music program at her new school.

   C She is quick to act in a time of crisis.

   D She is frustrated with her father.

4 From Elena's experience, readers may conclude that —

   F it's easy to adjust to a big change

   G everyone should learn to play an instrument

   H practice isn't always necessary to be good at something

   J confidence in yourself can come from unexpected experiences

> **Quick Tip**
>
> After reading a multiple-choice question, eliminate incorrect answers first. Then reread the text and look for evidence that will help you choose from the remaining responses.

EXTEND YOUR LEARNING

STRUCTURAL ELEMENTS OF A DRAMA

COLLABORATE

A drama is a story meant to be performed on a stage. Dramas contain **dialogue**, or the words characters say, and **stage directions** that describe the setting and the characters. A drama's plot is usually divided into one or more **acts** that are further separated into **scenes**.

Occasionally, important plot events may occur offstage after one scene ends and before the next begins. Readers can use details in the dialogue and stage directions to infer what happens between scenes.

- Reread "A Box of Ideas" on pages 210–213 in the **Literature Anthology**. Summarize what happens in each scene.

  In Scene 1, _____

  _____

  _____

  In Scene 2, _____

  _____

- How do you know how much time has passed between the two scenes?

  _____

- What has happened during that time? Explain how you know.

  _____

  _____

  _____

FORESHADOWING

COLLABORATE

Foreshadowing is a literary technique in which the author provides an early hint or suggestion of an event that will occur later in a story. Identifying the use of foreshadowing can help you predict how a plot will unfold.

An example of foreshadowing can be found in *Lizzie Bright and the Buckminster Boy* on **Literature Anthology** page 186. The narrator says, "And that was when he first heard the water ripping near him." This detail builds suspense because it hints, or foreshadows, that Turner will soon be facing an obstacle. The foreshadowing allows the reader pause to think about what that obstacle might be.

- Reread "Facing the Storm" on pages 2–5. Look for details that seem to hint at an event that might happen later. Then identify what actually happens. Record your ideas in the chart below.

Detail	What It Foreshadows	What Happens

CREATE A SIDEBAR

Sidebars are text features that add information about a topic or explain a related idea. They are usually set apart from the main text. For example, a sidebar might appear within a separate box on a page, or it may be in a different typeface.

- In *Stewards of the Environment* on **Literature Anthology** pages 214–217, you read about actions people take to promote a healthier environment.

- With a partner, think about how a sidebar might provide more information or explain a related idea in a section of *Stewards of the Environment*. Take notes below.

Main Text	Possible Sidebar
"Cleaner Rivers," page 215	
"Small Houses, Big Message," pages 215–216	
"Students Get an Environmental Education," page 216	

- Review your notes and choose one sidebar idea. Research the topic using a variety of print or digital sources. Use your research to write a sidebar that could be included in the text. Before you begin, complete the sentences below.

I will add a sidebar to the section _____

My sidebar will include details about _____

_____

ELEPHANT CAMP

Log onto **my.mheducation.com** and reread the *Time for Kids* online article "Elephant Camp," including the information found in the interactive elements. Then answer the questions below.

Time for Kids: "Elephant Camp"

- Why do Asian elephants need to be protected?

_____

_____

_____

- How does the author use a problem-and-solution text structure to organize information about elephants?

_____

_____

_____

_____

- Why do you think the Thai government has gone to such lengths in protecting elephants?

_____

_____

_____

_____

Unit 3 • Extend Your Learning   95

TRACK YOUR PROGRESS

WHAT DID YOU LEARN?

Use the rubric to evaluate yourself on the skills you learned in this unit.
Write your scores in the boxes below.

4	3	2	1
I can successfully identify all examples of this skill.	I can identify most examples of this skill.	I can identify a few examples of this skill.	I need to work more on this skill.

- [ ] Theme
- [ ] Sequence

- [ ] Context Clues
- [ ] Prefixes and Suffixes

- [ ] Main Idea and Key Details
- [ ] Synonyms and Antonyms

Something that I need to work more on is _____ because

_____

_____

Text to Self Think back over the texts that you have read in this unit.
Choose one text and write a short paragraph explaining a personal
connection that you have made to the text.

I made a personal connection to _____ because _____

_____

_____

_____

Present Your Work

COLLABORATE

Discuss how you will present your debate in support of whether mass transit or car travel is the better mode of transportation. Use the Presenting Checklist as you and your team practice your presentation. Discuss the sentence starters below and write your answers.

Presenting Checklist

☐ Time your rehearsals so that you know you'll be able to include your main points in the allotted time.

☐ Speak clearly and decisively, stressing the points you want the audience to remember.

☐ Make eye contact with individual members of the audience.

☐ Avoid comments unrelated to the topic.

One surprising piece of information I learned about modes of travel is

_____

_____

_____

I would like to know more about _____

_____

_____

filiphoto/Shutterstock

COLLABORATE

The paintings of Huang Guofu, a native of Chongqing, China, are assessed highly by art dealers and collectors from around the world. When Huang Guofu was just four years old, he lost his arms in an accident. At age 12, he began to paint using his right foot to hold the brush. He also paints with his mouth. Huang Guofu had to practice for a long time to perfect his craft. Because he worked hard to overcome such a challenge, he is quick to tell young people that there are no obstacles to prevent them from doing anything they want to do.

Look at the photograph. Turn to your partner and discuss qualities that help people overcome challenges they face. Write your ideas in the web.

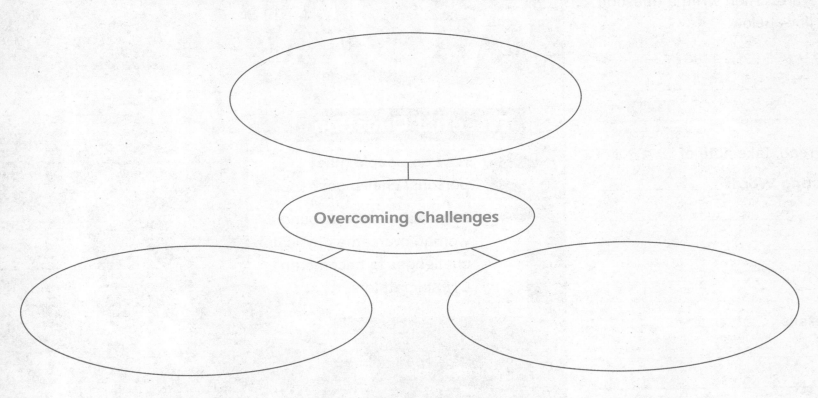

Overcoming Challenges

BLAST BACK!
studysync

Go online to **my.mheducation.com** and read the "Fancy Footwork" Blast. Think about the achievements people accomplish despite facing challenges. Why do you think those achievements are still prized? Then blast back your response.

SHARED READ

TAKE NOTES

Asking questions as you preview a text gives you a chance to think about what you already know about a topic and what you would like to learn. Before you read, look at the headings, photographs, and text features. Then write a question on the lines below.

_____
_____
_____

As you read, take note of

Interesting Words _____
_____
_____
_____

Key Details _____
_____
_____
_____

She Had to WALK Before She Could RUN

Essential Question

?

How do people meet personal challenges?

Read about how a young woman overcame physical challenges to become an Olympic athlete.

Wilma Rudolph at the 1960 Summer Olympics

Jerry Cooke/Corbis Historical/Getty Images

In a crowded Olympic stadium, the gun sounded and Wilma Rudolph took off like a bolt of lightning. As this amazing athlete ran confidently around the track, she never lost her cool. Sprinting toward the finish line, Rudolph used her **peripheral** vision to ensure that her competitors would not catch up. The crowd roared with elation as "the fastest woman in the world" finished more than three yards ahead of the other athletes.

Against All Odds

Though Wilma Rudolph inspired many during that 1960 Summer Olympics in Rome, Italy, her childhood had been riddled with hardships. Rudolph was one of 22 children born to an impoverished Tennessee family. While she was a toddler, her health **deteriorated** because of life-threatening illnesses.

When she was four years old, Rudolph contracted polio, a severe disease that causes paralysis. As a result, Rudolph lost the use of her left leg. Having polio could have been **devastating** for Rudolph. Instead, she faced this physical challenge with a positive attitude and never lost sight of her goal.

Rudolph's mother taught her very early to believe she could achieve any goal, and the first was to walk without leg braces. Once a week, she drove Rudolph 90 miles round-trip to Nashville for physical therapy. Her mother also instructed Rudolph's siblings on how to massage their sister's legs. Done several times a day, this monotonous routine continued for several years.

An Inspiring Comeback

Rudolph's doctors had little hope that she would ever be able to walk again. When she was nine years old, they decided to **assess** her progress. After the doctors removed the braces, they were amazed to see that Rudolph could walk on her own. They were stunned by what this young girl could do despite having contracted a crippling disease for which there was no cure.

FIND TEXT EVIDENCE

Read

Paragraph 1

Idioms

Underline clues that help you understand the meaning of "she never lost her cool." What does this tell you about Rudolph?

_____

_____

Paragraphs 2–5

Author's Point of View

What is the author's attitude toward Rudolph?

_____

_____

_____

Circle evidence that supports this point of view.

Reread

Author's Craft

Why might the author have included the information about Rudolph's mother and her siblings?

FIND TEXT EVIDENCE

Read

Paragraphs 1–2

Author's Point of View

Circle evidence that reveals the author's point of view about Rudolph's comeback from polio.

What is the author's point of view?

_____

_____

_____

Paragraphs 3–4

Reread

Underline text explaining struggles Rudolph faced in 1958 and 1959.

Reread

Author's Craft

How does the author organize details about Rudolph's challenges?

From then on, Rudolph never looked back. To **compensate** for the years she had been in braces, Rudolph became extremely active. As proof of her determination, she ran every day. She decided never to give up, no matter what happened.

Rudolph's brothers set up a basketball hoop in the backyard, and she and her siblings played all day. Rudolph became an avid basketball player at school, too. A track coach named Ed Temple from Tennessee State University spotted Rudolph at a basketball tournament and was extremely impressed by her athletic ability and **potential.** He invited her to attend a sports camp. Once again, Rudolph's life changed dramatically, this time for the better.

Rudolph displays her gold medals (above) at the 1960 games

An Olympic Champion

The minute Rudolph ran on a track, she loved it. When she was just sixteen years old, she qualified for the 1956 Summer Olympic Games in Melbourne, Australia. And Rudolph came home wearing the bronze medal she had won in the relay race.

After high school, Rudolph was awarded a full scholarship to major in education at Tennessee State University. But once again, Rudolph had to overcome challenges. In 1958, having put her shoulder to the wheel both in class and during track-and-field events, she became too ill to run. After she had a tonsillectomy, however, she felt better and started to run again. Unfortunately, Rudolph pulled a muscle at a track meet in 1959, and Coach Temple had to **implement** a plan for her recovery. Rudolph recovered just in time to qualify for the 1960 Summer Olympics in Rome.

Bettmann/Getty Images

Wilma Rudolph's Olympics Statistics

Date	Event	Time	Medal
1956	200 Meters	Not in finals	None
1956	4 x 100 Meters Relay	44.9 seconds	Bronze
1960	100 Meters	11.0 seconds	Gold
1960	200 Meters	24.0 seconds	Gold
1960	4 x 100 Meters Relay	44.5 seconds	Gold

In her individual sprints, Rudolph outshone her competition and won two gold medals with ease. During the relay event, however, the team comprised of four athletes from Tennessee State found themselves in hot water. After a poor baton pass, Rudolph had to pick up her pace and run like the wind to complete the last leg of the race. She successfully overtook Germany's last runner to win the race. Rudolph became the first American woman in track and field to win three gold medals. Of her feeling of accomplishment, she said she knew it was something "nobody could ever take away from me, ever."

Giving Back

The **summit** of Rudolph's career might have been her achievements as an Olympic athlete. Instead, she went on to accomplish much more. After graduating from college, she taught school and coached track. Soon Rudolph was traveling the country, giving speeches to school audiences.

To inspire others to do their best in spite of all challenges, she would note that "the triumph can't be had without the struggle." Rudolph achieved her dreams and, ever after, helped others to reach theirs.

> **Summarize**
>
> Use your notes and the photographs and table to write a summary of Wilma Rudolph's life and career. Cover the time period before, during, and after the 1960 Olympics.

FIND TEXT EVIDENCE

Read

Paragraph 1
Photographs and Tables

Circle the row in the table showing details about the 100 meter event. What new information do you learn?

_____

How does the photograph on page 102 support the information in the text and table?

_____

Paragraphs 2–3
Reread

Underline details that tell what Rudolph accomplished after her Olympic career.

Author's Craft

Why do you think the author ended the biography with a quote from Rudolph?

Vocabulary

Use the example sentences to talk with a partner about each word. Then answer the questions.

assess

Tests help teachers **assess** how well students are learning.

How do you assess your performance on a test?

_____

_____

compensate

On hot days, a fan can help **compensate** for the lack of a breeze.

How are the meanings of *compensate* and *replace* related?

_____

_____

deteriorated

My running shoes **deteriorated** after so many months of wear.

What is a synonym for *deteriorated*?

_____

_____

devastating

The **devastating** fire destroyed many trees.

What other natural occurrences can have devastating effects?

_____

_____

implement

My school plans to **implement** a program that promotes eating healthful foods.

What program do you think your school should implement?

_____

_____

 Build Your Word List Pick a word you found interesting in the selection you read. Use print or digital resources to look up the word's meaning, pronunciation, and part of speech and write them in your writer's notebook.

peripheral

The wide brim of her hat blocked some of her **peripheral** vision.

Why might peripheral vision be important?

_____

_____

_____

potential

The dark clouds indicate the **potential** for a rainstorm.

When is the potential for snow the greatest?

_____

_____

_____

summit

The climbers finally reached the **summit** of the mountain.

What is an antonym of _summit_?

_____

_____

_____

Idioms

The expression _it's raining cats and dogs_ is an idiom. An idiom is an expression whose meaning goes beyond the meaning of the individual words. Look for context clues to help you understand and verify the meanings of idioms you come across.

 **FIND TEXT EVIDENCE**

The phrase put her shoulder to the wheel _confuses me. Why would Rudolph place her shoulder against a wheel? But the sentence also says that Rudolph became too ill to run. I think the expression is an idiom that means "worked extremely hard."_

> In 1958, having <u>put her shoulder to the wheel</u> both in class and during track-and-field events, | she became too ill to run. |

Your Turn Use context clues to determine the meanings of these idioms in "She Had to Walk Before She Could Run."

Rudolph never looked back, _page 102_ _____

_____

found themselves in hot water, _page 103_ _____

_____

Reread

When you read a biography, you need to understand what the author thinks is important about each of the events in the subject's life. As you read "She Had to Walk Before She Could Run," you can pause to reread difficult sections to make sure you understand the author's points.

FIND TEXT EVIDENCE

You may need to reread the section "Against All Odds" on page 101 to make sure you understand the significance of what happened to Rudolph when she was a young child.

Quick Tip

The first sentence of a paragraph in nonfiction often introduces the topic of the paragraph. This is called a topic sentence. As you read, pay attention to how the details in the rest of the paragraph relate to the topic sentence.

Page 101

> Though Wilma Rudolph inspired many during that 1960 Summer Olympics in Rome, Italy, her childhood had been riddled with hardships. Rudolph was one of 22 children born to an impoverished Tennessee family. While she was a toddler, her health **deteriorated** because of life-threatening illnesses.
>
> When she was four years old, Rudolph contracted polio, a severe disease that causes paralysis. As a result, Rudolph lost the use of her left leg.

I read that Rudolph had poor health as a toddler and contracted polio at age four. That tells me that Rudolph's greatest challenges arose when she was still very young.

Your Turn How does the author show Rudolph's determination to overcome challenges at the 1960 Olympics? Reread paragraph 1 on page 103 to answer. As you read, remember to use the strategy Reread.

_____

_____

Photographs and Tables

"She Had to Walk Before She Could Run" is a biography. A biography often focuses on a certain time period or important aspect of the subject's life. It may include photographs as well as tables and other text features that add to your understanding of details in the text.

Quick Tip
When you look at a table, first read the title. Then review the heading of each column and row. Finally, look at the information across a row to compare the pieces of information.

 FIND TEXT EVIDENCE

This biography of Wilma Rudolph focuses on the ways she dealt with the difficult challenges she faced. The information in the table gives me specific details about her accomplishments.

Page 103

Wilma Rudolph's Olympics Statistics

Date	Event	Time	Medal
1956	200 Meters	Not in finals	None
1956	4 x 100 Meters Relay	44.9 seconds	Bronze
1960	100 Meters	11.0 seconds	Gold
1960	200 Meters	24.0 seconds	Gold
1960	4 x 100 Meters Relay	44.5 seconds	Gold

In her individual sprints, Rudolph outshone her competition and won two gold medals with ease. During the relay event, however, the team comprised of four athletes from Tennessee State found themselves in hot water. After a poor baton pass, Rudolph had to pick up her pace and run like the wind to complete the last leg of the race. She successfully overtook Germany's last runner to win the race. Rudolph became the first American woman in track and field to win three gold medals. Of her feeling of accomplishment, she said she knew it was something "nobody could ever take away from me, ever."

Giving Back

The **summit** of Rudolph's career might have been her achievements as an Olympic athlete. Instead, she went on to accomplish much more. After graduating from college, she taught school and coached track. Soon Rudolph was traveling the country, giving speeches to school audiences.

To inspire others to do their best in spite of all challenges, she would note that "the triumph can't be had without the struggle." Rudolph achieved her dreams and, ever after, helped others to reach theirs.

Summarize

Use your notes and the photographs and table to write a summary of Wilma Rudolph's life and career. Cover the time period before, during, and after the 1960 Olympics.

Tables

Tables show detailed information in an organized way.

Photographs

Photographs often show the subject at the time described.

 Your Turn Tell why the author chose to separate the information in the table from the main text.

_____

_____

_____

_____

Author's Point of View

The author of a biography usually expresses a personal point of view about the subject. Identifying this point of view can help you determine whether the author's assertions are backed by evidence or are unsupported.

 FIND TEXT EVIDENCE

As I reread "She Had to Walk Before She Could Run," I can look for details that reveal the author's attitude toward Wilma Rudolph. Then I can decide when statements about Rudolph are supported.

Details	Author's Point of View
The author refers to Rudolph as an "amazing athlete" at the Olympics.	
Rudolph faced the challenges of her illness with a "positive attitude."	

Your Turn Reread "She Had to Walk Before She Could Run." Identify more pieces of text evidence that convey the author's attitude toward Rudolph and add them to the graphic organizer on page 109. Then identify the author's point of view and explain how it is or is not supported by evidence.

> ### Quick Tip
>
> When you've completed your chart, look for text evidence that supports the author's assertions, or ideas. For example, both the table and the first paragraph on page 103 give specific examples supporting the assertion that Rudolph was an "amazing athlete" at the Olympics.

Details	Author's Point of View
The author refers to Rudolph as an "amazing athlete" at the Olympics.	
Rudolph faced the challenges of her illness with a "positive attitude."	

Respond to Reading

COLLABORATE

Discuss the prompt below. Think about how the author presents and describes the information. Use your notes and graphic organizer.

How does the author of "She Had to Walk Before She Could Run" help readers understand Wilma Rudolph's determination to be a great athlete?

_____

_____

_____

_____

_____

_____

_____

_____

_____

_____

_____

_____

_____

_____

Paraphrase Sources

When you **paraphrase** a source, you restate the information using your own words. An effective paraphrase conveys the meaning of the source without using the author's exact words. Claiming an author's words as your own is **plagiarism.** To avoid plagiarism, follow the tips below.

- Check to make sure your paraphrase is worded differently from the original text.
- Put quotation marks around any text taken directly from a source.
- Keep track of your sources so that you can properly cite them.

Why is it important to cite sources?

_____

_____

Record a Podcast With a partner or group, record a podcast about a person who has helped others overcome a challenge. Consider these questions when choosing and researching a subject:

- What inspired your subject to help others?
- Whom did your subject help?
- What did he or she do to help?

Discuss credible sources you might paraphrase and cite, as well as what music or other sound effects you may include. You will share your completed podcast with your classmates.

text from a source:

Helen Keller lost her senses of sight and hearing after suffering from an illness during infancy.

paraphrased text:

As an infant, an illness left

Helen Keller blind and deaf.

The sentence above shows how one student paraphrased a source's quotation to avoid plagiarism. Give an example of another way you could avoid plagiarizing the original.

_____

_____

_____

_____

_____

_____

_____

_____

Seeing Things His Own Way

Literature Anthology:
pages 256–267

? **How does the author's use of Erik's quote help you understand his character?**

Talk About It Reread paragraph 4 on **Literature Anthology** page 258. Talk with a partner about what Erik's quote means.

Cite Text Evidence What does Erik say that helps you understand his character? Write text evidence in the chart and tell why the author uses it.

 Synthesize Information

To determine the author's purpose for including Erik's quote, consider each sentence or phrase in the quote. Ask yourself, *What does this information tell me about Erik?* Then synthesize, or combine, these ideas into one new idea. Think about how this new idea describes Erik and why the author feels it's important for readers to understand.

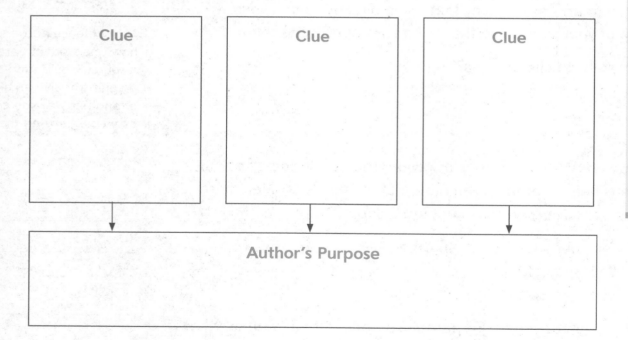

Clue	Clue	Clue

Author's Purpose

Write The author uses Erik's quote to help me understand that Erik is

_____

_____

How do you know that Erik's father played a big role in helping him achieve success in life?

 Talk About It Reread the last two paragraphs on **Literature Anthology** page 261. Talk with a partner about what Erik's father did after Erik's mother died.

Cite Text Evidence What did Erik's father do that helped Erik achieve success? Write text evidence in the chart.

 **Make Inferences**

Think about the qualities that drove Erik's father to plan adventurous trips for his family. What do they say about what Ed Weihenmayer is like? What do you think Erik learned from his father?

Text Evidence	Your Conclusion

Write I know that Erik's father played a big role in helping Erik succeed

because the author _____

_____

? **How does descriptive language help you visualize what mountain climbing was like for Erik?**

COLLABORATE

Talk About It Reread paragraph 2 on **Literature Anthology** page 264. Talk with a partner about the description of Erik's 1985 climb.

Cite Text Evidence What words and phrases tell about one of Erik's mountain climbing experiences? Write text evidence in the chart.

Quick Tip

As you read, stop after each description of what Erik does. What does each description show about the climb and what Erik learned on the climb? How does this information help you visualize Erik's climb?

Text Evidence

↓

Text Evidence

↓

Text Evidence

↓

What I Visualize

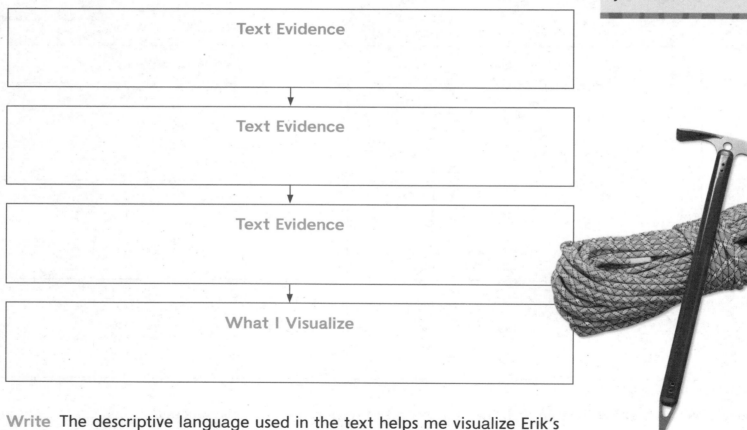

Write The descriptive language used in the text helps me visualize Erik's climb by _____

_____

Respond to Reading

COLLABORATE

Discuss the prompt below. Think about qualities that you find important in a role model. Use your notes and graphic organizer.

How does Marty Kaminsky convince you that Erik should be seen as a role model?

_____

_____

_____

_____

_____

_____

_____

_____

_____

_____

_____

_____

_____

_____

_____

Quick Tip

Use these sentence starters to talk about and cite text evidence.

Marty Kaminsky uses quotes to show . . .

He shares information about Erik's father to . . .

This makes it clear that . . .

Self-Selected Reading

Choose a text and fill in your writer's notebook with the title, author, and genre of the selection. Include a personal response to the text in your writer's notebook. A personal response might include an experience you had that is similar to what you read. It might also include how you feel about what you are reading.

Get Fit for Fun!

Literature Anthology pages 270–273

What Is Fitness?

[1]   Do you consider yourself fit? Being fit doesn't mean you need to spend every day running mile after mile. You don't need to be on any special diet, either. But nearly everyone can get into better shape with very little effort.

[2]   There are three main things you should do to be fit. First, it's important to be physically active. Second, eat a healthful diet. And third, maintain a healthy weight for your age and body type. It doesn't matter what your friends weigh!

[3]   As any athlete will tell you, there are degrees of fitness. You can probably walk a mile without getting winded, but could you run a mile? Can you climb several flights of stairs without stopping to catch your breath? Do you think you might eat too much junk food, such as chips, candy, or sugary sodas? Professional athletes must pay attention to diet and exercise to perform at their best, but nearly everybody can increase their regular physical activity and eat a balanced diet.

Reread paragraphs 1 and 2. In the margin or beside the text evidence, **number** the three things you can do to be fit. **Circle** the sentence that those clues support.

COLLABORATE

Reread paragraph 3. Talk with a partner about why the author is talking directly to the reader. **Underline** the sentences that support your discussion. Write the reasons here:

_____

_____

_____

_____

_____

Your Need for Water

1. Is all this talk of exercise making you thirsty? That's a good thing. In addition to a balanced diet, your body needs water to work properly. You use water to digest your food, to carry nutrients through your blood, to remove waste products, and to cool you through sweating.

Getting Started

2. It's easy to implement a fitness routine. Step away from the remote. Click off the computer. Get off the couch and get moving. Find an exercise buddy. And think about what to eat before you eat it.

3. How can you assess whether you're on the road to fitness? You'll have more energy and feel better.

In paragraph 1, **underline** text evidence that tells why you need water.

Talk with a partner about how the headings help you understand more about what you are reading.

Reread paragraphs 2 and 3. Why is "Getting Started" a good heading? **Make marks** in the margin beside text evidence that supports your answer. Write why here:

_____

_____

_____

_____

_____

_____

_____

? **How does the author help you understand how he or she feels about fitness?**

COLLABORATE

Talk About It Reread the excerpt on page 117. Talk with a partner about how the author feels about fitness.

Cite Text Evidence What words and phrases help you understand how the author feels about fitness? Write text evidence in the chart.

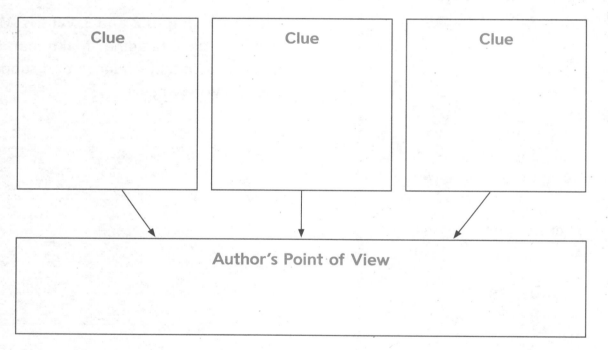

Clue	Clue	Clue

Author's Point of View

Write The author helps me understand how he or she feels about fitness

by _____

_____

_____

Author's Purpose

In an informational text, an author's purpose, or reason, for writing is often determined in part by the audience. For example, an author might think about the audience's prior knowledge of a topic. This helps the author decide what kinds of facts and examples to include in a text.

FIND TEXT EVIDENCE

In paragraph 2 of "Get Fit for Fun!" on page 116, the author claims there are three main components of physical fitness. The author's purpose is to inform a reader who may have limited knowledge on this topic. Here the author speaks directly to the reader and uses facts to back up the claim.

> There are three main things you should do to be fit. First, it's important to be physically active. Second, eat a healthful diet. And third, maintain a healthy weight for your age and body type. It doesn't matter what your friends weigh!

Your Turn Reread paragraph 3 of "Get Fit for Fun!" on page 116.

- Why does the author discuss athletes? _____

  _____

  _____

- Explain how this discussion helps the author inform readers about their own fitness. _____

  _____

Authors craft their texts to suit their purpose for writing. When you write an informative text, be sure to include facts, statistics, and examples that help your reader better understand the topic. Remember that even in informative writing, you should use language that will keep the audience engaged and interested.

Readers to Writers

Text Connections

? How does the way the poet and the authors of *Seeing Things His Own Way* and "Get Fit for Fun!" use words and phrases help you visualize the theme or message?

COLLABORATE

Talk About It The word *invictus* is a Latin word meaning "unconquered" or "invincible." Read the poem. Talk with a partner about why "Invictus" is a good title for the poem.

Cite Text Evidence **Underline** words and phrases in the poem that help you visualize how the speaker deals with the challenges he or she faces. **Circle** how the speaker feels about the challenges and about himself or herself.

Write The poet and authors use words and phrases to help me visualize _____

_____

_____

_____

_____

_____

_____

_____

Invictus

Out of the night that covers me,
Black as the pit from pole to pole,
I thank whatever gods may be
For my unconquerable soul.

In the fell clutch of circumstance
I have not winced nor cried aloud.
Under the bludgeonings of chance
My head is bloody, but unbowed.

Beyond this place of wrath and tears
Looms but the Horror of the shade,
And yet the menace of the years
Finds and shall find me unafraid.

It matters not how strait the gate,
How charged with punishments the scroll,
I am the master of my fate,
I am the captain of my soul.

— William Ernest Henley

SOCIAL STUDIES

Present Your Work

COLLABORATE

With your partner or group, discuss how you will present your podcast about a person who has helped others overcome a challenge. Use the Presenting Checklist as you practice your presentation. Discuss the sentence starters below and write your answers.

One interesting fact I learned while researching the life of my subject is

_____

_____

_____

This has inspired me to learn more about _____

_____

_____

_____

Tech Tip

You can present your podcast live to the class. If you are able to record your podcast for your presentation, review the audio to make sure it is clear and easy to understand. You may be able to edit out any interruptions or long pauses.

✓ Presenting Checklist

☐ Assign speaking roles and rehearse your presentation.

☐ Speak slowly, clearly, and with an appropriate volume.

☐ Remember that podcasting is usually an audio medium. Think about how you can adjust your voice or tone to add interest and keep listeners engaged.

☐ Listen to and respond politely to questions and comments from the audience.

LightFieldStudios/iStock/Getty Images

Expert Model

Literature Anthology: pages 256-267

Features of Biography

A biography is an account of a real person's life that is written by someone other than the subject. A biography

- informs about key events in the subject's life, especially challenges and achievements;

- communicates information about the subject's life in a logical order;

- features facts and relevant details to support the author's ideas about the subject's significance.

Word Wise

On page 258, the author describes the highest peak in North America as a place with *howling winds, freezing temperatures, sudden avalanches, devastating storms, deep crevasses,* and *gale-force winds.* Precise language grabs the reader's attention by painting a vivid and accurate picture of the setting.

Analyze an Expert Model Studying biographies will help you learn how to plan and write a biography. **Reread** page 258 of *Seeing Things His Own Way* in the **Literature Anthology**. Then answer the questions below.

How do you know the text is a biography? _____

_____

_____

_____

How does the author organize the information? _____

_____

_____

_____

Plan: Choose Your Topic

Quick Tip

In choosing your subject, think about historical figures, athletes, artists, and community or family members with interesting and inspiring lives. Choose someone you want to learn more about.

COLLABORATE

Brainstorm With a partner, brainstorm a list of people who overcame a challenge to achieve something important. Ask yourself: *What individual from the past or present has inspired me by his or her actions?* Write your ideas below.

_____

_____

_____

_____

Writing Prompt Choose one person who overcame a challenge from your list. Then write a biography about the person. Include supporting details that make it clear why the person is inspiring.

The subject of my biography will be _____.

Purpose and Audience Think about who will read or hear your biography. Will your primary, or main, purpose be to inform, persuade, or entertain your audience? How will you support the purpose of your essay?

My main purpose for writing is _____

I will use _____ to support the purpose of my essay.

Plan Ask yourself what you want readers to learn from your biography. You might ask: *What are the most significant events in my subject's life? What challenges did he or she face? Why is my subject inspirational?* Write your ideas in your writer's notebook.

Plan: Focus on a Person

Research Use the questions you wrote in your writer's notebook to guide your research. Search for answers in books, articles, interviews, and websites. Take notes on key details that describe significant events and accomplishments. Remember to record why the events and accomplishments in your subject's life are important, and how your subject overcame challenges he or she faced.

List two important events or accomplishments from your subject's life that you want to focus on in your biography.

1 _____

_____

2 _____

_____

Cite Your Sources To avoid plagiarism, write down each source's author, title, and publication information. Use this information to prepare a bibliography. Here is a sample entry for a book about whales:
Ahab, Robert. *Atlantic Whales*. Boston: Melville Press, 2015.

Graphic Organizer In your writer's notebook, make a Details and Conclusion chart to organize the information in your biography. Use the details to help you conclude why your subject's accomplishments are significant.

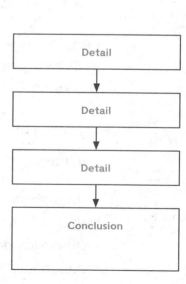

Detail

Detail

Detail

Conclusion

Digital Tools

For information on citing sources, review a Sample Works Cited Page. Go to **my.mheducation.com**.

Draft

Supporting Details Biographers support their writing with facts, examples, quotations, and other relevant details. In the excerpt below from "She Had to Walk Before She Could Run," the author notes that Rudolph met with hardship as a child. The author supports that statement with facts and details about specific challenges Rudolph faced.

> Though Wilma Rudolph inspired many during that 1960 Summer Olympics in Rome, Italy, her childhood had been riddled with hardships. Rudolph was one of 22 children born to an impoverished Tennessee family. While she was a toddler, her health deteriorated because of life-threatening illnesses.

Now use the excerpt above as a model to write a paragraph for your biography. State an important idea about your subject. Then provide details from your research to support that idea.

_____

_____

_____

_____

_____

Write a Draft Use your Details and Conclusion chart to help you write your draft in your writer's notebook. Begin by introducing your subject. Be sure your conclusion reminds readers why he or she is inspirational.

Revise

Logical Order It's important to present the events in your subject's life in a logical order to help readers understand the relationship between events and when things happened. Transition words and phrases can help clarify the order in which events happened and the relationships between events or ideas. Read the paragraph below. Then revise it to present the information in a logical order.

> The Wright brothers successfully tested their flying machine. It was a cold and windy day in December of 1903. They had many unsuccessful attempts at flight in the years leading up to this day. They continued to improve their design until they succeeded.

_____

_____

_____

_____

_____

Revision As you revise your draft, make sure your events are described in a logical order. Add transitions as needed to clarify the order in which events happened and the relationships between events or ideas.

Peer Conferences

COLLABORATE

Review a Draft Listen carefully as a partner reads his or her work aloud. Take notes about what you liked and what was difficult to follow. Begin by telling what you liked about the draft. Ask questions that will help the writer think more about the writing. Make suggestions that you think will make the writing stronger. Use these sentence starters.

I enjoyed this part of your draft because . . .

The order of your events would be more logical if . . .

I have a question about . . .

Have you considered adding a detail about . . . ?

Partner Feedback After your partner gives you feedback on your draft, write one of the suggestions that you will use in your revision. Refer to the rubric on page 129 as you give feedback.

Based on my partner's feedback, I will _____

_____

_____

After you finish giving each other feedback, reflect on the peer conference. What was helpful? What might you do differently next time?

Revision As you revise your draft, use the Revising Checklist to help you figure out what text you may need to move, elaborate on, or delete. Remember to use the rubric on page 129 to help you with your revision.

✓ Revising Checklist

☐ Does my biography make it clear why my subject is inspirational?

☐ Do I have enough details to support my ideas about my subject?

☐ Are my facts and details relevant and from reliable sources?

☐ Have I organized the information in a logical order that is easy to understand?

☐ Have I used transitions to show a logical sequence of events?

Edit and Proofread

When you **edit** and **proofread** your writing, you look for and correct mistakes in spelling, punctuation, capitalization, and grammar. Reading through a revised draft multiple times can help you make sure you're noticing any errors. Use the checklist below to edit your writing.

Tech Tip

Grammar checkers do not always detect incomplete sentences or sentence fragments. As you edit, make sure all your sentences contain a subject and a verb. One way to identify sentence fragments is by reading your writing aloud and listening for sentences that are missing an important piece of information, such as the subject, the verb, or both.

✓ Editing Checklist

☐ Are names, places, dates, and other proper nouns capitalized?

☐ Do all sentences express a complete thought?

☐ Are possessive pronouns used correctly?

☐ Are all quotations punctuated correctly, with quotation marks?

☐ Are all words spelled correctly?

List two mistakes you found as you proofread your biography.

1 _____

_____

2 _____

_____

Publish, Present, and Evaluate

Publishing When you **publish** your writing, you create a clean, neat final copy that is free of mistakes. If you are writing in cursive, write legibly and leave space between words. Consider including photographs or video clips of your subject to add multimedia elements to your biography.

Presentation When you are ready to **present** your work, rehearse your presentation. Use the Presenting Checklist to help you.

Evaluate After you publish your writing, use the rubric below to **evaluate** your writing.

What did you do successfully? _____

What needs more work? _____

_____

✓ Presenting Checklist

☐ Make eye contact with your audience.

☐ Speak clearly, slowly, and with an appropriate volume.

☐ Speak expressively and use an appropriate tone.

☐ Listen actively and respond politely to comments and questions.

4	3	2	1
• focuses on a subject's life, how he or she overcame a challenge, and why he or she is inspirational • clearly supports the important ideas and events with facts and details from research • orders all events logically and includes transitions to clarify order	• focuses on a subject's life but lacks information on how the challenge was overcome or why the subject is inspirational • mostly supports the important ideas with facts and details from research • orders most events logically and includes some transitions to clarify order	• focuses on a subject's life but does not include how the subject overcame a challenge or why he or she is inspirational • provides some support of important ideas and events, but not entirely from research • order of events is somewhat logical, but few transitions are used	• is unfocused and does not reflect details about a specific subject's challenges or why the subject is inspirational • does not provide support for ideas and events • does not present events in a logical order, and does not use transitions

Talk About It

Essential Question

When are decisions hard to make?

COLLABORATE

Have you ever had to make a difficult decision? The student in this photo must decide among several options for his project. Each choice will entail interviewing people in his community. But what to choose? Choosing a topic he feels comfortable with would make it easier for him to conduct interviews. But maybe that's *too* easy. What if, instead, he chose an unfamiliar topic? Choosing the unfamiliar can sometimes be the most interesting choice!

Talk to a partner about what you know about making difficult decisions. What do you think about when making a decision? Write your ideas in the web.

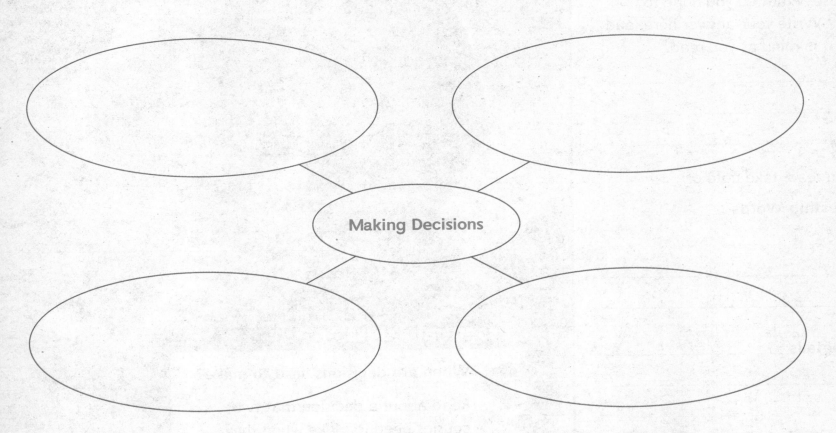

Making Decisions

BLAST BACK!

studysync

Go online to **my.mheducation.com** and read the "Decisions, Decisions" Blast. Think about what you know about the challenges of making decisions. What can help people make decisions? Then blast back your response.

TAKE NOTES

Establishing a purpose for reading helps you focus on and remember what happens in a drama or other narrative. Preview the title and the character descriptions in the cast list to help you determine a purpose. What do you hope to learn? Write your answer here, and keep it in mind as you read.

_____

_____

_____

As you read, take note of

Interesting Words _____

_____

_____

Key Details _____

_____

_____

_____

Treasure in the Attic

Cast of Characters
LIZ, a 12-year-old girl
EMMA, Liz's cousin, age 11
MR. SNOW, a shopkeeper
YARD SALE CUSTOMER

Essential Question

? **When are decisions hard to make?**

Read about a decision that two cousins need to make when they discover a long-lost family heirloom.

Tristan Elwell

SCENE 1 *The attic of Liz's house; Liz and Emma are kneeling.*

Emma (*looking through a box*): We'll never get through all this stuff!

Liz: We have to. I need twenty-five more dollars for that new bike. My dad says we can sell at a yard sale anything we find up here. You can keep half of whatever we make.

Emma (*coughing*): I know. I just didn't realize it would **entail** breathing in so much dust.

Liz (*with enthusiasm*): I don't think anyone has looked at Grandpa and Grandma's stuff since they moved to Florida. There's a **multitude** of treasures up here.

Emma: Be on the lookout for a pair of pearl earrings. Grandma says Great-Grandma forgot what she did with them. You're supposed to inherit them, since you're the oldest heir among the grandkids.

Liz: Wow. I hope they're worth a lot of money!

Emma: If I had something of Great-Grandma's, I'd never sell it.

Liz (*finding an old diary, flipping pages*): Wow, a diary! Listen to this: (*reading*) "October 7, 1936. I feel such **empathy** for Anna Snow and her family. They may have to leave us to find work elsewhere. This terrible Depression has bred such suffering for our neighbors. We are fortunate that Albert's income is not solely dependent on local business. My new **endeavor** is to be Anna's **benefactor**. If I gave her my pearl earrings, Anna could sell them to pay debts. She'd surely do the same for me. But can I? Albert would never approve if I gave away his wedding gift to me. Yet I must do it! It will be our secret—Anna's and mine. . .."

Emma (*excitedly*): So that's what happened to Great-Grandma's earrings! Anna Snow must have been a wonderful friend. Could hers be the same family that owns Snow's General Store?

Liz: Let's go find out.

DRAMA

FIND TEXT EVIDENCE

Read

Page 133

Theme

Underline dialogue that tells what each character would do with the earrings.

Summarize

Summarize what happened to the earrings.

_____

_____

_____

Reread

Author's Craft

How does the author help you understand the cousins' perspectives on the earrings?

Fluency

With a partner, read aloud the parts of Emma and Liz with appropriate expression.

SHARED READ

FIND TEXT EVIDENCE 🔍

Read

▼

Page 134

Scenes

Circle the text that tells where Scene 2 takes place.

Homophones

Draw a box around a clue in Scene 2 that helps you tell the difference between *morning* and *mourning*. Write their meanings.

_____

_____

_____

Stage Directions

Underline how Emma speaks to Mr. Snow. What does this tell you about her?

_____

Reread

Author's Craft

How does the author use details in Scene 2 to build suspense?

SCENE 2 *Snow's General Store; enter Liz and Emma.*

Mr. Snow: Good morning. May I help you young ladies?

Emma (*tentatively*): Um. . . Mr. Snow, we were wondering if you might be related to Anna Snow.

Mr. Snow: Yes, I'm her grandson. Why do you ask?

Liz: We're trying to solve a mystery. Our great-grandmother, Flossie Howard, was a good friend of your grandmother's. She wrote about her in a diary she kept. (*She shows the diary to Mr. Snow.*)

Mr. Snow: Flossie Howard, you say? That name rings a bell, but I can't quite place it. There were lots of Howards in town in those days.

Liz (*with disappointment*): Well. . . thanks anyway.

Mr. Snow: I do hope you solve your mystery.

SCENE 3 *Liz's yard, a few days later; the girls are setting items out for the yard sale as neighbors arrive.*

Tristan Elwell

Emma: Look, Liz. Isn't that Mr. Snow from the store? I wonder what he's doing here.

Mr. Snow: Hello, girls. I think this might belong to you. (*He hands Liz a small yellowed envelope.*)

Liz (*reading*): "For Flossie."

Mr. Snow: I knew I'd heard that name somewhere. After you left, I found that envelope tucked away in the back of the store safe.

Liz (*opens the envelope, finds a note and the pearl earrings; reading*): "Dearest Flossie, I can't tell you how much I appreciate the gesture. But I can't accept this kindest of offers. The earrings are yours and too lovely to part with."

Mr. Snow: Her brother Bert took charge of the store when she and Granddad left. In all the hubbub, I guess she forgot she'd stowed the earrings in the safe. And she never did come back.

Liz: Even so, they've been secure all these years. Thanks very much, Mr. Snow.

Yard Sale Customer: Those earrings are lovely. Would you take twenty-five dollars for them?

Liz: Twenty-five dollars? I could get my new bike.

Emma: But the earrings are family heirlooms! And we don't even know what they're worth.

Liz (*to herself, seized by indecision*): I'd really like the money for the bike. But. . . maybe Emma's right. They *are* Great-Grandma's earrings. (*to Yard Sale Customer*) Sorry, ma'am, they're not for sale. (*to Emma*) We should each keep one. I'll earn money for the bike some other way. Hey, I'll bet the *basement* could use an **extensive** cleaning out!

Summarize

Use your notes to summarize the important events in the play. When you summarize, be sure to maintain the meaning of each event and retell events in a logical order.

FIND TEXT EVIDENCE

Read

Page 135

Summarize

How do the girls end up with the earrings? Summarize what happened.

_____

_____

_____

Theme

Underline text evidence that reveals what Liz decides to do with the earrings and why she does so. What lesson does she learn?

_____

_____

Reread

Author's Craft

Why does the author include the words *seized by indecision* in the stage directions of Liz's last dialogue?

Vocabulary

Use the example sentences to talk with a partner about each word. Then answer the questions.

benefactor

A wealthy **benefactor** gave our school a large donation.

What is one decision a benefactor must make?

_____

_____

empathy

I moved to a different school last year, so I have **empathy** for the new student's uncertainty.

How are the meanings of *empathy* and *understanding* related?

_____

_____

endeavor

Jackie loves adventure, so her next **endeavor** will be climbing a mountain.

What new endeavor would you like to try?

_____

_____

entail

Swimming the 200-meter race in less than two minutes would **entail** a lot of training.

What preparation does getting good grades entail?

_____

_____

extensive

The big storm caused **extensive** damage to the town's park.

Where could you find an extensive collection of books?

_____

_____

 Build Your Word List Pick a word you found interesting in the selection you read. Make a word web showing different forms of the word. Define each form using an online or print dictionary, and then write a sentence for each.

indecision

My **indecision** about what to wear makes me late some mornings.

Describe a situation when you experienced indecision.

_____

_____

_____

multitude

They saw a **multitude** of birds nearly covering the beach.

Where might you see a multitude of people?

_____

_____

_____

tentatively

I **tentatively** dipped my toe in the cold water.

What else might a person do tentatively?

_____

_____

_____

Homophones

Homophones are words that sound the same but have different meanings and are often spelled differently. You can use context clues to help choose the correct meaning. A dictionary can also verify the meaning, pronunciation, and part of speech of a homophone.

🔍 FIND TEXT EVIDENCE

I know that a homophone of pair *is* pear. *Since the text refers to earrings, the meaning of* pair *in this sentence must be "two of something," not "a fruit."*

Be on the lookout for a pair of pearl earrings.

Your Turn Use context clues to tell the meaning of the words from "Treasure in the Attic" and their homophones.

heir, *page 133,* and **air** _____

_____

_____

right, *page 135,* and **write** _____

_____

_____

Summarize

You can summarize a play just as you would a story. Doing so helps you understand and remember important plot events. Pause after reading each of the three scenes in "Treasure in the Attic" to review the key events.

 FIND TEXT EVIDENCE

Reread all of Scene 1 on page 133. Identify key details and use them to retell in your own words what is most important in this scene.

> Page 133
>
> **Liz** (*with enthusiasm*): I don't think anyone has looked at Grandpa's and Grandma's stuff since they moved to Florida. There's a **multitude** of treasures up here.
>
> **Emma:** Be on the lookout for a pair of pearl earrings. Grandma says Great-Grandma forgot what she did with them. You're supposed to inherit them, since you're the oldest heir among the grandkids.

 Your Turn Summarize Scene 2 on page 134.

_____

_____

_____

_____

_____

I read that two cousins are looking for things to "sell at a yard sale." Liz finds their great-grandma's diary, and they read about earrings they know have been missing. I can summarize this scene by saying that while looking for things to sell at a yard sale, Liz and Emma stumble upon a mystery they want to solve about their great-grandma's missing earrings.

Quick Tip

Taking notes while you are reading will help you summarize a scene in a play. Include

- the characters;
- the setting;
- the main events;
- the conflict, or problem;
- the resolution.

When you summarize, make sure to describe the events in order.

Structural Elements

The selection "Treasure in the Attic" is a play, or a work to perform on stage. A play is written as lines of dialogue to be spoken aloud. It has stage directions to indicate setting and action. It may have acts, or long sections, and scenes, or short sections.

FIND TEXT EVIDENCE

"Treasure in the Attic" is a play in three scenes. Stage directions in italics tell where each scene takes place and how characters speak.

Page 133

SCENE 1 *The attic of Liz's house; Liz and Emma are kneeling.*

Emma (*looking through a box*): We'll never get through all this stuff!

Liz: We have to. I need twenty-five more dollars for that new bike. My dad says we can sell at a yard sale anything we find up here. You can keep half of whatever we make.

Emma (*coughing*): I know. I just didn't realize it would **entail** breathing in so much dust.

Liz (*with enthusiasm*): I don't think anyone has looked at Grandpa and Grandma's stuff since they moved to Florida. There's a **multitude** of treasures up here.

Emma: Be on the lookout for a pair of pearl earrings. Grandma says Great-Grandma forgot what she did with them. You're supposed to inherit them, since you're the oldest heir among the grandkids.

Liz: Wow. I hope they're worth a lot of money!

Emma: If I had something of Great-Grandma's, I'd never sell it.

Liz (*finding an old diary, flipping pages*): Wow, a diary! Listen to this: (*reading*) "October 7, 1936. I feel such **empathy** for Anna Snow and her family. They may have to leave us to find work elsewhere. This terrible Depression has bred such suffering for our neighbors. We are fortunate that Albert's income is not solely dependent on local business. My new **endeavor** is to be Anna's **benefactor**. If I gave her my pearl earrings, Anna could sell them to pay debts. She'd surely do the same for me. But can I? Albert would never approve if I gave away his wedding gift to me. Yet I must do it! It will be our secret—Anna's and mine. . . ."

Emma (*excitedly*): So that's what happened to Great-Grandma's earrings! Anna Snow must have been a wonderful friend. Could hers be the same family that owns Snow's General Store?

Liz: Let's go find out.

Scenes
A scene is what happens during one particular time and in one setting.

Stage Directions
Stage directions describe the setting and characters' actions. They are not spoken by the actors.

Readers to Writers

Stage directions often help the actor know how the character is feeling. The same piece of dialogue can be said in different ways. Liz talks about her grandparents' belongings "with enthusiasm." We know she is happy about what she finds. Imagine how different this part of the scene would be if her dialogue was said in a sad tone.

Your Turn Why is the action in "Treasure in the Attic" divided in three scenes? How do the stage directions help you visualize what happens in each scene?

COLLABORATE

_____

_____

_____

Theme

To determine a theme, or central message, of a play, pay attention to the dialogue and stage directions. Think about what causes the characters to say what they say. Consider what the characters have learned, and how they change as result of what happens to them, to help you infer a theme.

🔍 FIND TEXT EVIDENCE

When I reread Scene 1 of "Treasure in the Attic," I think about what effect Liz's hopes for buying a new bike may have on her decisions later in the play. The girls' reactions to reading their great-grandmother's diary also help me understand the characters.

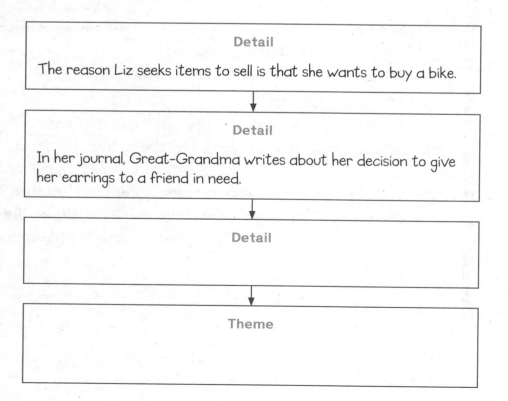

> **Detail**
>
> The reason Liz seeks items to sell is that she wants to buy a bike.

↓

> **Detail**
>
> In her journal, Great-Grandma writes about her decision to give her earrings to a friend in need.

↓

> **Detail**

↓

> **Theme**

COLLABORATE

Your Turn Reread the play. Complete the graphic organizer on page 141 with additional details about what the characters do and say. Then use all of the details to determine a theme of the play.

Detail

The reason Liz seeks items to sell is that she wants to buy a bike.

↓

Detail

In her journal, Great-Grandma writes about her decision to give her earrings to a friend in need.

↓

Detail

↓

Detail

↓

Theme

Respond to Reading

Discuss the prompt below. Think about how the author indicates what the characters are thinking and feeling. Use your notes and graphic organizer.

How does the author help you understand why Liz decides not to sell her great-grandmother's earrings?

_____

_____

_____

_____

_____

_____

_____

_____

_____

_____

_____

_____

_____

_____

Quick Tip

Use these sentence starters to discuss the text and to organize ideas.

- _Liz's dialogue shows . . ._
- _The author includes stage directions that . . ._
- _At the beginning of the play, Liz . . . By the end of the play . . ._

Grammar Connections

As you write, check for subject-verb agreement. A compound subject, such as _Liz and Emma,_ is treated like a plural subject.
Incorrect: _Liz and Emma looks for the earrings._
Correct: _Liz and Emma look for the earrings._

Story Mapping

A **story map** allows an author to keep track of the different elements of a story. It helps an author arrange all the pieces of the story into an engaging narrative. Use these tips to create your own story map:

- List the story's characters and its setting, or time and place.
- Note the conflict, or problem, the characters will face. This will often involve a difficult decision that the main character must make.
- Add specific events that will develop the plot of your story, bring it to a climax, and eventually resolve the conflict.

How can story mapping help you organize your ideas? _____

_____

_____

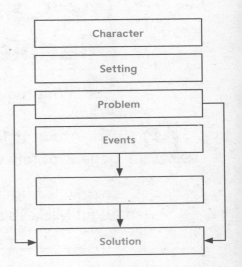

There are many different kinds of story maps a writer can use to organize information. Here is one option a student used to begin mapping a story. As part of your research for your graphic organizer, look online for other options to consider.

Make a Graphic Novel With a partner or small group, research characters from Greek mythology. Then choose one character and create a short graphic novel in which he or she must make a difficult decision. Your story should include

- the problem the character faces;
- the options available and the possible consequences of each choice;
- the outcome of the decision and how the character feels about it.

Discuss how you will illustrate your graphic novel. You may wish to find examples of graphic novels in print or online to use as a model. You will be sharing your graphic novel with your classmates.

The Case of the Magic Marker Mischief Maker

Literature Anthology: pages 274–283

? **What do the stage directions tell you about how Mickey feels?**

Talk About It Reread the stage directions on **Literature Anthology** page 275. Talk with a partner about what Mickey does and how he acts.

Cite Text Evidence Record text evidence from the stage directions that tell about Mickey's character. Write what you can conclude from the clues.

Make Inferences

Characters in a play don't always state their feelings outright. Instead, readers must use stage directions and dialogue to infer how a character feels. Pay attention to Mickey's stage directions and dialogue. What is he doing? What kind of language does he use when speaking with Principal Abrego? What does this tell you about how Mickey feels about the principal?

| Clue |
| Clue |
| Clue |
| Conclusion |

Write The stage directions help me _____

_____

? How does the author use what the characters say to create conflict?

COLLABORATE

Talk About It Reread the first column on **Literature Anthology** page 276. Talk with a partner about the conversation between Mickey and Principal Abrego.

Cite Text Evidence What words does the author use to show conflict between the characters? Write text evidence in the chart.

Text Evidence	How It Shows Conflict

Write The author uses what the characters say to create conflict by _____

_____

_____

? How does the author use what Bucho says to help you understand Bucho's character?

Talk About It Reread Act 2, Scene 2 on **Literature Anthology** page 280. Talk with a partner about what you learned about Bucho's personality from what he says.

Cite Text Evidence What words and phrases help you know what Bucho is like? Write text evidence and explain what it says about Bucho.

What Bucho Says	What It Shows

Write The author helps me understand what Bucho is like by _____

_____

_____

Quick Tip

In a play, a character's words do not appear in quotation marks. Instead, they are labeled with the character's name. This makes it easy to scan the text and identify dialogue a certain character says.

Evaluate Information

Evaluating details is particularly helpful when you are reading a mystery because it helps you identify clues that might point to the mystery's solution. Reread Bucho's dialogue and think carefully about his words. Do they make him seem guilty or innocent? Why?

Respond to Reading

COLLABORATE

Discuss the prompt below. Think about what Mickey must keep in mind as a detective. Use your notes and graphic organizer.

How does the author use conflict to help you understand the decisions Mickey makes?

_____

_____

_____

_____

_____

_____

_____

_____

_____

_____

_____

_____

_____

_____

_____

Self-Selected Reading

Choose a text and fill in your writer's notebook with the title, author, and genre of the selection. Include a personal response to the text in your writer's notebook. If you are reading a mystery, you might explain how you thought the mystery would be solved and how your prediction compared to what actually happened.

Dramatic Decisions: Theater Through the Ages

Literature Anthology:
pages 286–289

Kabuki Theater

1   On the other side of the world at about the same time, another new theatrical style was developing in Japan. Called "kabuki," it began in the early 1600s with female casts. Soon, however, the actors were all males. Kabuki performances entail extravagant makeup and costumes and include dancing and singing.

2   One of the greatest kabuki playwrights is Chikamatsu Monzaemon. His play *Sonezaki Shinju*, which was published in 1720, has a plot that is similar to *Romeo and Juliet*. In it two young people are in love, but circumstances prevent them from being together. Audiences identify with them as they unsuccessfully try to follow their hearts and make a desperate decision to escape together.

Reread paragraph 1. **Circle** the sentence that tells you what the paragraph is about. Write it on the lines below.

_____

_____

_____

_____

Underline clues in paragraph 1 that describe kabuki theater.

COLLABORATE

Reread paragraph 2. Talk with a partner about how the author helps you understand what the play *Sonezaki Shinju* is about. **Draw a box** around text evidence in the paragraph that supports your discussion.

Modern American Theater

3   In 1736, the Dock Street Theatre in Charles-Towne, South Carolina—now called Charleston—was built. It was the first building in the North American colonies erected solely to be a theater. Today, actors perform in theaters everywhere across the country, from the great stages of New York to small community theaters. But some aspects of the experience have never changed, including the popularity of plays in which characters are faced with difficult decisions to make.

4   One very popular modern American play is *A Raisin in the Sun* by Lorraine Hansberry. The play centers on the Youngers, an African-American family on the South Side of Chicago. Set in the 1950s, the story dramatizes the difficult choice faced by the family, which is about to receive a large sum of money. The adult Youngers have different ideas about what to do with the money. Each person's idea is valid, but each has a different goal—and it excludes the others. In the end, decisions are made and problems are resolved as the characters hoped they would be.

Reread paragraph 3. **Circle** something about the theater experience that hasn't changed over time.

COLLABORATE

Reread paragraph 4. **Underline** how the author supports the text you circled in paragraph 3. Talk with a partner about *A Raisin in the Sun*. Why does the author refer to this play?

_____

_____

_____

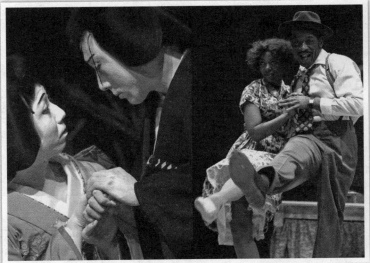

? How does the way the author organizes information help you understand the history of theater?

COLLABORATE

Talk About It Reread the excerpts and headings on pages 148 and 149. Talk about how the author helps you understand the history of theater.

Cite Text Evidence How does the author organize the information? Write text evidence to support how it helps you understand the topic.

Text Evidence

↓

How It Helps

Write The author helps me understand the history of theater by _____

_____

_____

You can often use headings to better understand how the text is organized. For example, the heading on page 148 indicates that the section is about kabuki, a Japanese form of theater. The word *modern* in the heading on page 149 indicates that the section contains information about recent theater. That points to the author's use of sequence to structure the text and organize details about the history of theater.

Imagery

Imagery is the author's use of specific language to help readers visualize the people, places, ideas, and events of a text. Authors often use sensory language, words and phrases that appeal to the reader's senses, to create imagery. Imagery also contributes to the mood, or feeling, of a text.

 FIND TEXT EVIDENCE

In the first lines of "Dramatic Decisions" on **Literature Anthology** page 286, imagery helps the reader visualize the start of a theatrical performance. Words and phrases such as *hush, darkened*, and *an actor's voice fills the air* communicate the audience's experience at the start of a play.

> A hush falls over the darkened room. The crowd is alert with anticipation, their eyes focused on the stage. As an actor's voice fills the air, the audience relaxes, settling back in their seats and ready to be entertained.

COLLABORATE

Your Turn Reread the second paragraph on page 287.

- How does the author help you visualize ancient Greek amphitheaters?

  _____

  _____

- How does imagery help the author make the text more engaging?

  _____

  _____

Precise words are the key to creating imagery. The more specific an author's description, the easier it is for readers to visualize what you're describing. As you revise your writing, think of words that appeal to a reader's sense of sight, hearing, touch, smell, or taste. A print or online thesaurus can help you choose more precise language.

Text Connections

? **How do the photographer and the authors of *The Case of the Magic Marker Mischief Maker* and "Dramatic Decisions: Theater Through the Ages" portray difficult decisions characters may face in drama?**

Talk About It Look at the photograph and read the caption. Talk with a partner about what you see in the photograph. Identify the people and discuss each person's role.

Cite Text Evidence **Circle** clues in the photograph that show how performers decide to portray characters on stage. **Underline** evidence in the caption that supports your answer.

Write The ways the photographer and authors portray decisions are similar in that _____

_____

_____

_____

_____

_____

The actors rehearse a scene from their upcoming play. The play's director helps them decide how to portray the characters.

Present Your Work

COLLABORATE

Discuss with your group how you will present your graphic novel about a character from Greek mythology. Use the Presenting Checklist as you practice your presentation. Discuss the sentence starters below and write your answers.

After researching the decisions made by mythological characters, I understood that _____

_____

_____.

Now i would like to learn _____

_____

_____.

Hill Street Studios/Blend Images/Getty Images

Quick Tip

Consider performing your graphic novel by having different members of your group read the various roles. You may also want to use a digital slideshow to display each individual panel of your graphic novel as you present it.

✔ Presenting Checklist

☐ Make sure your graphic novel is clearly visible to your audience. If possible, have copies available for your classmates.

☐ Make sure everyone in your group has a role in the presentation.

☐ As you present your work, explain how the text and illustrations of the graphic novel relate to each other.

☐ Listen carefully and respond politely to comments from your audience.

Think of a time when you had an obligation to take responsibility for something you had done. Perhaps you smacked a home run through your neighbor's window, like in the photograph. Perhaps your actions accidentally caused damage or hurt someone's feelings. How did you respond?

Look at the photograph. Talk to a partner about what you see. How can the person who caused the damage take responsibility for it? Fill in the web with examples of what it means to take responsibility for your actions.

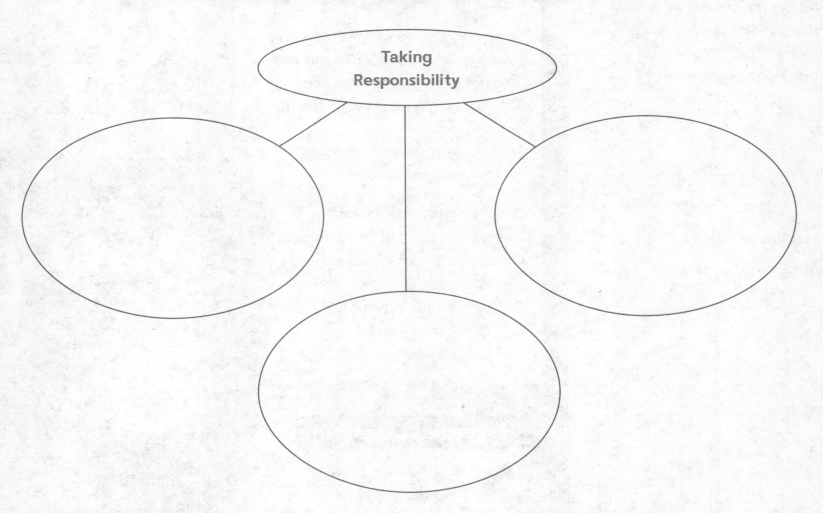

Taking
Responsibility

Go online to **my.mheducation.com** and read the "Solutions" Blast. Think about what you know about volunteering. How might volunteering be a good way to take responsibility? Then blast back your response.

Steve Bronstein/Stone+/Getty Images

TAKE NOTES

Before you read, preview the poems. Read the titles and look at the photographs to predict what you think the poems will be about. Write your predictions below. Remember to confirm or revise your predictions as you read.

_____

_____

_____

_____

As you read, take note of

Interesting Words _____

_____

_____

_____

Key Details _____

_____

_____

_____

_____

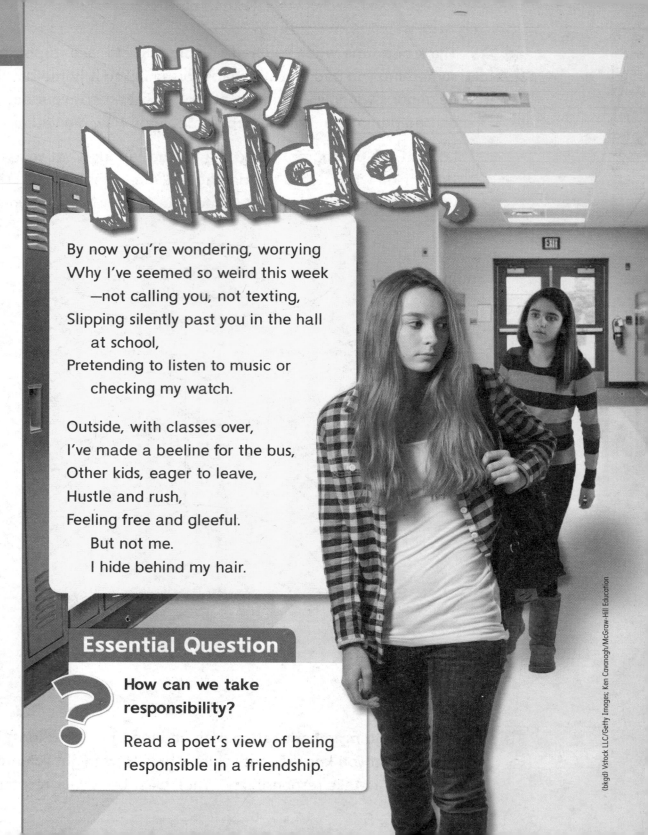

Hey Nilda,

By now you're wondering, worrying
Why I've seemed so weird this week
　—not calling you, not texting,
Slipping silently past you in the hall
　at school,
Pretending to listen to music or
　checking my watch.

Outside, with classes over,
I've made a beeline for the bus,
Other kids, eager to leave,
Hustle and rush,
Feeling free and gleeful.
　But not me.
　I hide behind my hair.

Essential Question

?

How can we take responsibility?

Read a poet's view of being responsible in a friendship.

(bkgd) Vstock LLC/Getty Images; Ken Cavanagh/McGraw-Hill Education

Here at home, my secret doesn't sit so well.
Once you know what I did,
You'll see red.
I know I'm answerable to you,
I have an obligation to make it right.
So here's what happened:
You think someone stole your camera . . .
No, I borrowed it without asking—
    Just to try it out, but
    Then I lost it.

I looked, looked, looked
In the laugh-loud cafeteria, the echo-hollow gym,
The bottom of my crammed and
    messy locker,
The plastic couches in the teachers' lounge,
And the shush-quiet aisles of the library—
Every place I could think of.
And it's gone.
My fault.
I'll give you my allowance for
    the next few months.
But I wonder—can money
    mend a friendship?

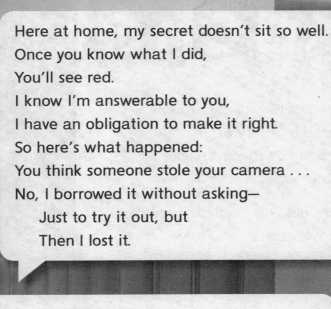

(bkgd) Ingram Publishing; Ken Cavanagh/McGraw-Hill Education

FIND TEXT EVIDENCE 🔍

Read

Page 156
Point of View

How does the speaker feel about the situation?

_____

_____

Underline details that helped you find your answer.

Page 157
Alliteration

Circle words in the first two lines of the last stanza that repeat the same beginning consonant sound. What does this repetition achieve?

_____

_____

Reread

Author's Craft

How does the author help you visualize and understand the events in the poem?

FIND TEXT EVIDENCE

Read

Page 158

Assonance

Circle words in the fourth line of the first stanza that share the same vowel sound.

Point of View

Who is the speaker of the poem? How does she feel? **Underline** text evidence that supports your answer.

_____

_____

_____

Make Inferences

What can you infer about the girls' friendship and why?

_____

_____

Reread

Author's Craft

How do details in the photograph convey the speaker's point of view?

Hi Rachel,

Yep, you're right.
I wondered why you were walking around
Like you were scared or angry or
As if you'd been crying or trying to hide,
—Or all of the above.

Good thing I wasn't holding anything breakable
When I read your message,
Because I might have dropped it
—Or flung it across the room.

Instead, I dropped down into our rickety recliner
And clenched my teeth tight,
My body shaking as hard
As if I were outside
Wearing shorts in the freezing rain.

I mean, come on!
You borrowed my new camera
without asking?
Then let me think it was stolen?
I thought I could trust you.
And I thought you would trust me enough
To tell me the truth.

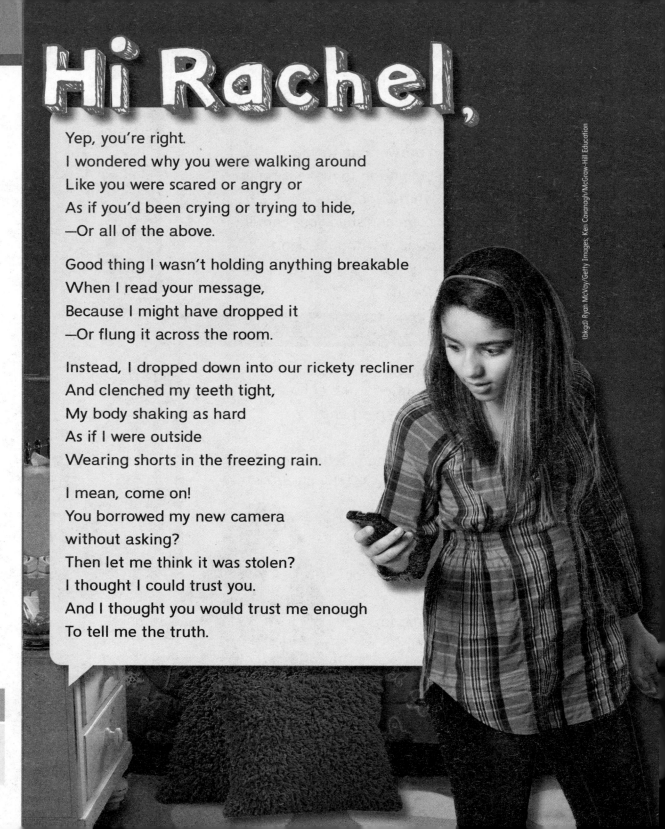

How long have we been friends?
Since we were five, that's how long.
We may not see eye-to-eye at times,
But we have always been honest
—With each other.

Just so you know:
I found my camera yesterday,
Stuck in a big box with some
    socks in the lost and found.

Let's not blow this out of
    proportion,
Maybe just treat it as water
    under the bridge.
Start again, okay?
Still friends?
I hope so.
I've got two tickets to Friday's
    concert, and
I don't want to go by myself.

Nilda
—Lareine Interne

Make Connections

Describe a time when you took
responsibility for your actions in
a friendship.

Talk about whether your predictions
on page 156 were confirmed.

FIND TEXT EVIDENCE

Read
Page 159
Narrative Poetry

How do you know this is a narrative
poem, or a poem that tells a story?

_____

_____

_____

Figurative Language

Underline clues that hint at the
meaning of "water under the
bridge" in the seventh stanza. Why
does Nilda use this expression?

_____

_____

Reread
Author's Craft

Why is the poet's use of messages
an effective way to structure the
two poems?

(bkgd) Ingram Publishing; Ken Cavanagh/McGraw-Hill Education

Vocabulary

Use the example sentences to talk with a partner about each word. Then answer the questions.

answerable

The soccer players are **answerable** to the coach for their actions during the game.

To whom are you answerable at school?

_____

_____

lounge

The patient waited in the **lounge** outside the doctor's office.

Where else might you wait in a lounge?

_____

_____

obligation

I have an **obligation** to make sure my dog is walked and fed.

What is a synonym for *obligation*?

_____

_____

proportion

A puppy's paws are large in **proportion** to its legs.

How would you describe an owl's eyes in proportion to its head?

_____

_____

Poetry Terms

free verse

Free verse poems don't rhyme and often sound like normal speech.

How is a free verse poem different from a sonnet?

_____

_____

narrative poem

In a **narrative poem**, the poet tells a story in verse form.

What elements besides a plot would you expect to find in a narrative poem?

_____

_____

alliteration

A poem that includes **alliteration** groups words that begin with the same sound.

Give an example of alliteration.

_____

_____

assonance

Assonance is the repetition of a vowel sound in words that are near each other in a poem.

Why might a poet use assonance?

_____

_____

_____

> **Build Your Word List** Find a word in "Hey Nilda" or "Hi Rachel" that signals a precise action, emotion, or state of being. Write the words, their definitions, and pronunciations in your writer's notebook.

Figurative Language

An **idiomatic expression** is a phrase with a figurative, rather than literal, meaning. In a poem, idioms such as _talk a mile a minute_ can make the speaker's words sound like everyday speech. Use context clues to identify the meaning of an idiomatic expression.

🔍 FIND TEXT EVIDENCE

In "Hey Nilda," the idiom see red _doesn't refer to literally seeing the color red. The phrases_ Once you know what I did _and_ I'm answerable to you _tell me that the speaker is nervous about how her friend will react. So_ see red _must refer to great anger._

Once you know what I did,
You'll see red.
I know I'm answerable to you,
I have an obligation to make it right.

Your Turn Find an idiomatic expression in "Hi Rachel." Identify its meaning and write it below.

_____

_____

_____

_____

Ken Cavanagh/McGraw-Hill Education

Alliteration and Assonance

Quick Tip

Assonance and rhyme feature words with the same sounds. Assonance can appear anywhere in a line of poetry, while rhyme appears often at the ends of lines.

Alliteration is the repetition of a consonant sound at the beginnings of words that are near one another. **Assonance** is the repetition of a vowel sound within a group of words. Poets use these devices to add a song-like quality to a poem and to draw attention to certain feelings or ideas.

FIND TEXT EVIDENCE

Reread "Hey Nilda" on pages 156–157. Look for examples of alliteration and assonance. Think about what they tell you about Rachel's state of mind.

Page 156

By now you're wondering, worrying
Why I've seemed so weird this week
  —not calling you, not texting,
Slipping silently past you in the hall
  at school,
Pretending to listen to music or
  checking my watch.

Repeating the w *sound at the beginnings of words and the long* e *sound within words draws attention to the tension and worry that Rachel is feeling about what has happened.*

Your Turn Find an example of alliteration and one of assonance in "Hi Rachel" on pages 158–159. Tell how they draw attention to feelings or ideas.

1 _____

_____

2 _____

_____

Free Verse and Narrative

Free verse poetry has no set rhyme, meter, or line length. This may make it sound like everyday speech. Imagery and descriptive language are common in free verse. **Narrative** poetry tells a story in verse form with characters, a setting, and a plot. It may or may not be written in free verse.

FIND TEXT EVIDENCE

I can tell that "Hey Nilda" is free verse because it doesn't contain a pattern of rhyming words or stressed syllables. It sounds similar to regular speech. It is also a narrative poem because it tells a story. The poet's word choice helps me visualize events in the plot.

Page 156

"Hey Nilda" is a free verse narrative poem. It tells a story without a set rhyme or meter.

Your Turn Reread "Hi Rachel" on pages 158–159. Is the narrative poem "Hi Rachel" also free verse? Why or why not?

Readers to Writers

When writing about a poem, be careful to not confuse the poet and the speaker. The poet is the poem's author and makes decisions about the poem's form. The speaker is the narrative voice created by the poet. Thoughts, ideas, and feelings expressed in a poem belong to the speaker, and not necessarily to the poet.

Point of View

In a narrative poem, as in fiction, the story may be told by one of the characters. That character is known as the speaker of the poem. The poet uses the first-person point of view of the speaker to express a particular perspective, feeling, or idea.

 FIND TEXT EVIDENCE

As I reread "Hey Nilda," I notice that the speaker, Rachel, uses the first-person pronouns I, me, *and* my. *The use of these pronouns tells me that the events in this narrative poem are described from Rachel's perspective.*

> **Quick Tip**
>
> As in fiction, pronouns can signal the point of view in a narrative poem. When the speaker uses pronouns such as *I*, *me*, and *my*, he or she is describing events from a first-person point of view. As you reread, look for sentences with first-person pronouns for clues to the speaker's feelings and perspective.

Details	Point of View
The speaker, Rachel, is telling the story.	The story is told from the speaker's point of view. Rachel is the speaker. Through the words, we learn that Rachel feels guilty and is afraid that her actions have ruined her friendship with Nilda.
The speaker uses the pronouns "I," "me," and "my."	
The speaker tells Nilda that she's been avoiding her.	
The speaker admits that she lost Nilda's camera.	
The speaker says she wants to make it up to Nilda.	

 Your Turn Reread "Hi Rachel." In the graphic organizer on page 165 list key details that help you identify who is telling the story and what feelings and ideas are being expressed.

Details	Point of View

Respond to Reading

COLLABORATE

Discuss the prompt below. Think about the events that develop the
conflict and lead to a resolution. Use your notes and graphic organizer.

In the narrative poems "Hey Nilda" and "Hi Rachel," how does the poet
use point of view to develop the main conflict and its resolution?

_____

_____

_____

_____

_____

_____

_____

_____

_____

_____

_____

_____

_____

_____

_____

Formatting an Email

An **email** is a quick and easy way to communicate with a business, government leader, or organization. When writing an email to an organization, follow this format:

- To: (organization's email address)
- Subject: (a word or phrase that identifies your topic)
- a message that states your reason for writing

How would an email to an organization differ from a message you might send a friend?

_____

_____

Write an Email With a partner, create an email to a volunteer organization that interests you. In your email, express your interest in the organization and request information about joining it. Consider the following points:

- Why does the organization interest you?
- How would you like to participate?
- Who is the best person at the organization to contact for your question, and how should this person be addressed?

Discuss how you will research your organization so you have accurate information to include in your email. After you complete your email, you will present it to your class.

```
To: volunteers@example.web

Subject: Volunteering


To the Volunteer Coordinator:

We are students in Ms. Suarez's
sixth-grade class at River
Middle School. We would like to
participate in this year's
spring project. Can you please
tell us how old one must be to
volunteer?

Sincerely,

Kara Stephens and Kameel Jordan
```

An email to an organization should include formal language. Notice the formal greeting in the sample above.

 Tech Tip

Volunteer organizations often have websites and email addresses ending in *.org*. Like *.gov* (government) and *.edu* (schools), a *.org* email address tells you that this is not a personal or business address.

*Literature Anthology:
pages 290–292*

This Is Just to Say
to Mrs. Garcia, in the office

**? How can you use the voice of each speaker to compare the
two poems?**

Talk About It Reread the poems on **Literature Anthology** pages 290–291.
Talk with a partner about language in each poem that helps you describe
the voice, or personality, of each speaker.

Cite Text Evidence What words and phrases help you understand each
poem's voice? Write text evidence and tell how the poems are different.

Page 290	Page 291	How They Are Different

Write I can identify the voice of each poem and compare them by _____

_____

_____

_____

to Thomas

? **How does the poet's choice of words help you understand Mrs. Garcia's perspective, or viewpoint?**

Talk About It Reread "to Thomas" on **Literature Anthology** page 292. Talk with a partner about how Mrs. Garcia responds to what Thomas has done.

Cite Text Evidence What clues in the poem show Mrs. Garcia's perspective? Write text evidence in the chart.

Text Evidence

↓

Perspective

Write The poet helps me understand Mrs. Garcia's perspective by _____

_____

_____

Respond to Reading

Discuss the prompt below. Think about the theme, or message, of each poem. Then think about how the voice in each poem contributes to the theme. Use your notes and graphic organizer.

How do the poets use voice to help you understand the themes of their poems?

_____

_____

_____

_____

_____

_____

_____

_____

_____

_____

_____

_____

_____

Quick Tip

Use these sentence starters to talk about and cite text evidence.

- *Each poet creates a mood by . . .*
- *The poets use voice to show . . .*
- *This helps me understand the themes of the poems by . . .*

Self-Selected Reading

Choose a text and fill in your writer's notebook with the title, author, and genre. Include a personal response to the text in your writer's notebook. When you make a personal connection, you might think of an experience you had that is similar to what you read.

Primer Lesson

 How does descriptive language in "Primer Lesson" help you understand the poem's message?

Literature Anthology: pages 294–295

Talk About It Reread "Primer Lesson" on **Literature Anthology** page 294. Talk with a partner about what the speaker says about proud words.

Cite Text Evidence What words and phrases tell what the speaker wants you to know about using proud words? Write text evidence.

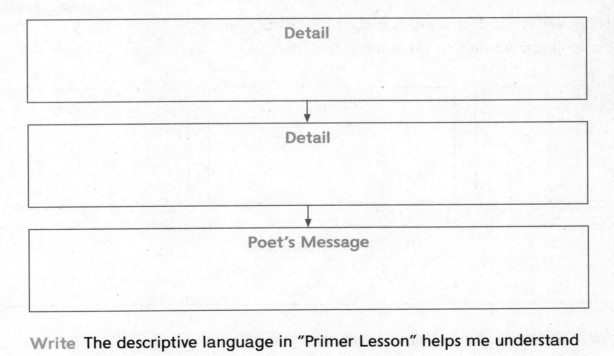

Detail

↓

Detail

↓

Poet's Message

> ## Quick Tip
>
> The word *proud* can have a positive connotation, or feeling, when it refers to self-respect. It can also have a negative connotation, or feeling, such as when it refers to someone showing scorn or arrogance.

Write The descriptive language in "Primer Lesson" helps me understand

_____

_____

_____

If I can stop one Heart from breaking

? How do the imagery and word choice in "If I can stop one Heart from breaking" help you understand the speaker's feelings?

Talk About It Reread "If I can stop one Heart from breaking" on **Literature Anthology** page 295. Talk with a partner about the speaker's feelings, or attitude, about helping others.

Cite Text Evidence What words and phrases does the speaker use to express his or her feelings? Write text evidence in the chart.

Evaluate Information

Compare the wishes the speaker shares in the first stanza of the poem to those expressed in the second stanza. What do the actions the speaker describes in the second stanza tell you about what he or she thinks is important in life?

Clue	Clue	Clue

How the Speaker Feels

Write The imagery and word choice help readers understand the speaker's feelings by _____

_____

_____

Tone

Tone is the speaker's attitude or feeling toward a topic. In a poem word choice and line length contribute to tone. Sound devices such as rhyme, rhythm, repetition, and alliteration also help create tone.

FIND TEXT EVIDENCE

In "Primer Lesson" on **Literature Anthology** page 294, the speaker begins and ends with a clear warning to readers: "Look out how you use proud words." In between those lines, the speaker uses words that suggest stern images such as "long boots, hard boots," "walk off proud," and "they can't hear you." These images and the repeated warning communicate a serious, authoritative tone.

Your Turn Reread "If I can stop one Heart from breaking" on Literature Anthology page 295.

- How does Dickinson use repetition in the poem? Explain what the repetition might mean. _____

  _____

  _____

- How does this repetition help the speaker express a specific tone?

  _____

  _____

  _____

Readers to Writers

Tone can change within a poem. For example, the tone might start out worried, become upset, and end up being cheerful or hopeful. To help you check your tone when you write, think about the speaker's attitude. If the speaker's attitude changes, so should the tone in the poem.

Text Connections

? How is the way the illustrator shows the theme of taking responsibility similar to the way the poets write about taking responsibility in the poems you read this week?

Talk About It Look at the illustration. Talk with a partner about what the girl is doing. Discuss what that reveals about the girl's character.

Cite Text Evidence **Circle** clues that help you understand how the girl in the illustration is taking responsibility and meeting an obligation. Think about how speakers such as Thomas and Mrs. Garcia feel about taking responsibility. Talk about how words and actions show how people can be responsible for how they treat others.

Write The illustrator shows a form of responsibility similar to the poems because _____

_____

_____

_____

_____

_____

_____

Catherine Lane/iStock/Getty Images Plus/Getty Images

Expression and Phrasing

Before you read a poem aloud, identify what it expresses. That will help you read the poem with **expression** and bring life to the speaker's feelings and thoughts. Also look for commas, dashes, and other punctuation marks that indicate **phrasing**, or when to pause as you read. Paying attention to phrasing can also make the poem's meaning clearer.

> Page 157
>
> No, I borrowed it without asking—
>   Just to try it out, but
>   Then I lost it.

The dash and comma in the poem signal places to pause while reading.

COLLABORATE

Your Turn Turn back to page 159. Take turns reading aloud the last stanza of "Hi Rachel" with a partner. Pay attention to punctuation. Think about the feelings the speaker expresses. Show these feelings in the way you read the poem.

Afterward, think about how you did. Complete the sentences below.

I remembered to _____

_____

Next time, I will _____

_____

Expert Model

Literature Anthology: pages 290-292

Features of a Free Verse Narrative Poem

A free verse narrative poem is a poem that tells a story. It does not usually use rhyme, meter, or regular line lengths. A free verse narrative poem

- has characters and a plot with a logical sequence of events;

- uses imagery to help readers visualize the story;

- often has a tone that expresses the speaker's attitude toward the subject or what's happening.

Word Wise

Notice how the lines in the poem are broken up. This focuses the reader on certain actions, images, and feelings. For example, "I have stolen" focuses the reader on the fact that Thomas stole something before telling what he stole. This emphasizes that the act of stealing is more important than what Thomas stole.

Analyze an Expert Model Studying other free verse narrative poems will help you learn how to plan and write one of your own. **Reread** "to Mrs. Garcia, in the office" on **Literature Anthology** page 291. Write your answers to the questions below.

Give an example of imagery from "to Mrs. Garcia, in the office." Why do you think the poet uses this imagery? _____

_____

_____

How does Thomas feel about having stolen the doughnuts? How do you know? _____

_____

_____

Plan: Choose Your Topic

Freewrite Think about a problem common to kids, such as arguments with friends, managing after-school time, or having to do something new and difficult. How might the problem be resolved? On a separate piece of paper, quickly write your ideas without stopping. Then discuss your ideas with a partner.

Writing Prompt Use your ideas to write a free verse narrative poem about a problem and how it was resolved.

I will write about _____

_____

_____

Purpose and Audience What is your purpose—to inform, persuade, or entertain? Is there a theme or message you want your audience to understand? Who will read or listen to your poem?

My purpose is to _____

My audience will be _____

Plan Think about the identity of the poem's speaker. Is the speaker telling about himself or herself, or is the speaker telling about other people? How does the speaker feel about the problem and how it was solved? Respond in your writer's notebook.

Plan: Sequence of Events

Logical Order Like any other narrative, the events in a free verse narrative poem should follow a logical order. Readers need to be able to follow what is happening and why it is happening. As you plan your poem's sequence of events, consider these questions:

- What caused the problem? What were the consequences of the problem? How was the problem solved? What happened after the problem was solved?

- Am I describing events in an order that's logical and easy to follow? Do I need to use transition words such as *before that, then,* or *later*?

Give details about two sequential events in your narrative.

1 _____

_____

2 _____

_____

 Graphic Organizer In your writer's notebook, make a Sequence of Events chart. Fill in the events that happen at the beginning, middle, and end of your free verse narrative poem.

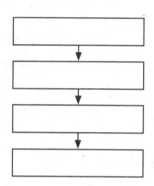

Draft

Imagery Authors use imagery to help readers visualize the details in a piece of writing and understand the feelings attached to them. Precise words, sensory details, and figurative language help create vivid imagery. Read the lines from "Hi Rachel" below. Think about how the writer uses imagery. Why is "clenched my teeth tight" a stronger image than "kept my mouth closed"?

> Instead, I dropped down into our rickety recliner
> And clenched my teeth tight,
> My body shaking as hard
> As if I were outside
> Wearing shorts in the freezing rain.

Now use the lines above as a model as you write lines that could go in your own free verse narrative poem. Include an example of imagery.

_____

_____

_____

_____

_____

 Write a Draft Use your Sequence of Events chart to help you write your draft in your writer's notebook. Check that your events tell a clear story about a problem and a solution.

Revise

Tone In poetry, tone is the speaker's attitude toward the subject. Ways to create tone in a free verse poem include the use of descriptive words and phrases, repetition, alliteration, and assonance. Read the lines below. Rewrite them to clearly express a tone. How would you describe that tone? Write it below your poem.

> I was supposed to help you study.
>
> But I forgot.
>
> I know it was wrong.

The following lines have an unclear tone:

The sun came up. It was a new day.

To convey a hopeful tone, the lines can be rewritten:

The sun bloomed golden on the horizon, casting a brilliant light upon the new day.

_____

_____

_____

_____

These lines have a _____ tone.

Revision As you revise your draft, think about how to use tone to best convey the speaker's attitude.

Peer Conferences

COLLABORATE

Review a Draft Listen carefully as a partner reads his or her work aloud. Take notes about what you liked and what was difficult to follow. Begin by telling what you liked about the draft. Ask questions that will help the writer think more about the writing. Make suggestions that you think will make the writing stronger. Use these sentence starters:

I enjoyed this part of your draft because . . .

More imagery in this stanza would help me visualize . . .

I wasn't clear about the sequence of events when . . .

I think the tone would be clearer if you . . .

Partner Feedback After your partner gives you feedback on your draft, write one of the suggestions that you will use in your revision. Refer to the rubric on page 183 as you give feedback.

Based on my partner's feedback, I will _____

_____

_____

After you finish giving each other feedback, reflect on the peer conference. What was helpful? What might you do differently next time?

Revision As you revise your draft, use the Revising Checklist to help you figure out what text you may need to move, elaborate on, or delete. Remember to use the rubric on page 183 to help you with your revision.

✓ Revising Checklist

- ☐ Does my poem tell a story about a problem and how it is solved?
- ☐ Would adding more imagery help readers better visualize the events?
- ☐ Would rearranging events or adding transitions help make the sequence clearer?
- ☐ Are there places where I could add or replace a word to more clearly convey tone?

Tech Tip

Spelling and grammar checkers are not always accurate when you use them with poetry. They will often highlight words, punctuation, and spelling that you are deliberately using in an unusual way. Think about the effect on your poem of each correction the checker suggests before you ignore or make a change.

Edit and Proofread

When you **edit** and **proofread** your writing, you look for and correct mistakes in spelling, punctuation, capitalization, and grammar. Reading through a revised draft multiple times can help you make sure you're correcting any errors. Use the checklist below to edit your sentences.

✓ Editing Checklist

- ☐ Is all punctuation used thoughtfully and correctly?
- ☐ Do all pronouns refer clearly to a noun?
- ☐ Are all pronouns used in the proper case?
- ☐ Are all proper nouns, including names and locations, capitalized?
- ☐ Are all words spelled correctly?

Grammar Connections

The rules of grammar and punctuation are often relaxed in poetry. Because a free verse poem is less structured and sounds more conversational than a traditional poem, it may include run-on sentences and sentence fragments. It may also use dashes or commas or no punctuation at all at the ends of lines. Edit and proofread your punctuation thoughtfully to let readers know when to pause as they read your poem.

List two mistakes you found as you proofread your free verse narrative poem.

1 _____

_____

2 _____

_____

Publish, Present, and Evaluate

Publishing When you **publish** your writing, you create a clean, neat final copy that is free of mistakes. Consider whether or not you want to add any illustrations to your poem.

Presentation When you are ready to **present** your work, rehearse your presentation. Use the Presenting Checklist to help you.

Evaluate After you publish your writing, use the rubric below to **evaluate** your writing.

What did you do successfully? _____

What needs more work? _____

_____

✓ Presenting Checklist

- ☐ Stand up straight.
- ☐ Take a deep breath to steady your voice before you begin speaking.
- ☐ Look at the audience.
- ☐ Use your voice expressively to convey the feelings in your poem.
- ☐ Speak at a rate and volume that reflect the tone of your poem.

4	3	2	1
• the poem tells an engaging narrative about a problem and solution • the events are told in a clear, logical order • effectively uses words to convey a specific tone and create vivid imagery	• the poem tells a narrative about a problem and solution • adequately tells a sequence of events in a logical order • chooses some words to convey a tone and create imagery	• the poem tells about a problem and solution but is not a narrative, or story • the sequence of events is somewhat unclear or illogical • the tone is unclear or there is little imagery	• the poem is not a narrative and does not tell about a problem or solution • does not tell about an event • does not convey a tone or create imagery

Spiral Review

You have learned new skills and strategies in Unit 4 that will help you read more critically. Now it is time to practice what you have learned.

- Author's Point of View
- Idioms
- Structural Elements
- Make Inferences
- Theme

Connect to Content

- Primary and Secondary Sources
- Figurative Language

Read the selection and choose the best answer to each question.

Patsy T. Mink:

★★★★★★★★★★★★★★★★★★★★★★★★★★★★★★★

CIVIL RIGHTS HERO

Patsy Takemoto Mink stands in front of the U.S. Capitol after becoming the first Asian American woman elected to the House of Representatives.

[1]　When Patsy Takemoto Mink was a teenager, she played basketball for her high school team in Hawaii. However, it was the 1940s, and her school thought girls weren't strong enough to play on a full court. She and her teammates could only play on a half court.

[2]　Her experience on the basketball court was one of many experiences that led Patsy T. Mink to recognize widespread inequality in the United States. She saw firsthand how people received unequal treatment because of their race or gender. This started Mink on a journey to fight unjust rules and laws that led to her becoming the first Asian American woman in Congress.

Discrimination in College

[3]　One of Mink's early fights against inequality began when she was in college. Student housing at the time was racially segregated. Knowing segregation was wrong, she organized a group of people to fight the policy. The group was successful, and the university changed its rules.

[4]　After earning a degree in zoology and chemistry, Mink applied to medical school. She was rejected by every school to which she applied. Mink believed she was rejected because of her gender. This led her to decide to become a lawyer so she could further her fight to change laws and end discrimination.

Elected Office

[5]   With a law degree, Mink felt ready to run for office. She was elected to the Hawaii Territorial Legislature in 1956 and to the Hawaii Senate in 1958. In 1964, she was elected to the U.S. House of Representatives. She was the first Asian American woman in the House, where she served for a total of 24 years.

Mother of Title IX

[6]   Mink said, "We have to build things that we want to see accomplished, in life and in our country, based on our own personal experiences." Mink's experiences inspired her to build protections against discrimination. The Civil Rights Act of 1964 outlawed discrimination based on race and religion, but Mink felt more was needed to protect women's rights. She wrote the Women's Educational Equity Act, known as Title IX. The law prevents gender discrimination in school programs. It ensures everyone, regardless of gender, has the same opportunities in sports and education.

Honors

[7]   Patsy T. Mink was influential in getting Title IX passed. For this reason, President George W. Bush renamed it the Patsy T. Mink Equal Opportunity in Education Act following Mink's death in 2002. In addition, Mink was elected to the National Women's Hall of Fame. These are well-deserved honors for a woman who devoted her life to fighting for equal rights.

Mink (top) wrote a law that has helped <u>level the playing field</u> by giving opportunities to female athletes like American soccer champion Alex Morgan (bottom).

(t) Douglas Graham/Congressional Quarterly/Getty Images; (b) Daniel Bartel/Icon Sportswire/Getty Images

SHOW WHAT YOU LEARNED

1 What can you infer from the information in paragraph 4?

A Becoming a lawyer is easier than becoming a doctor.

B Medical schools accept more students now than they did years ago.

C Excellent grades are required to get into medical school.

D Years ago, medical schools discriminated against female students.

2 What does <u>level the playing field</u> mean in the caption on page 185?

F increase the amount of

G give everyone an equal chance

H destroy what had been built

J make something more difficult

Quick Tip

Reread the caption and look for context clues that point to the meaning of the idiom. Which answer choice do the clues best support?

3 What can you infer from the information in paragraph 5?

A A law degree is not very useful for lawmakers and politicians.

B Mink had to run for office many times before being elected.

C Mink was reelected to the House of Representatives several times.

D A law degree is required to run for elected office.

4 Which statement from the text shows the author's point of view?

F Student housing at the time was racially segregated.

G Mink believed she was rejected because of her gender.

H The law prevents gender discrimination in school programs.

J These are well-deserved honors for a woman who devoted her life to fighting for equal rights.

Read the selection and choose the best answer to each question.

Lost and Found

Cast of Characters
Agnes and **Keith**: Twelve-year-old twins
Mom: The twins' mother

Scene 1: *The twins' backyard. Mom is building a cabinet. There are building materials and tools nearby. She looks up as the twins join her in the yard.*

Agnes: What are you making?

Mom: A cabinet for my new client.

Keith: It looks great. Very impressive, Mom.

Mom: You want to see how I'm building it? I can teach you guys.

(Agnes and Keith look at each other. They are not eager to do this.)

Keith: Maybe another time.

Mom (*sighs and gives a little smile*): That's what you two always say. But I'll keep asking. Maybe one day you'll say yes, you never know.

(The twins smile and walk away.)

Scene 2: *The next day. Agnes's bedroom. The room is very messy with clothes, art materials, and other things belonging to Agnes scattered everywhere. Agnes is looking a bit panicked as she searches for something. She gets down on the floor and looks under the bed. At the sound of footsteps approaching, Agnes leaps up, grabs a book, and sits on the bed, pretending to be reading.*

Keith (*walks into the bedroom holding a small box and wrapping paper and then stops near the bed, surprised to see what Agnes is reading*): I thought you already read that book, Agnes.

Agnes: I'm reading it again.

Keith: But you hated it. You said it was one of the worst books you ever read.

Agnes: Yeah, well, just giving it a second chance.

Keith: Okay. Whatever. Anyway, remember, Dad planned a special night tonight to thank Mom for all she does for us. He's been cooking all day. And I found this box. It's perfect for the bracelet we made her.

Agnes: Maybe Mom doesn't want a bracelet.

Keith (*confused*): What are you talking about? She loves bracelets.

Agnes (*pauses before speaking*): You're going to be really mad. Promise you won't be mad.

(Keith, concerned, looks at Agnes without speaking.)

Agnes: I can't find the bracelet. I've looked everywhere.

Keith: Well, maybe if your room wasn't such a mess! What if we can't find it in time? Or at all? We need to make another plan.

Agnes: I'm really, really sorry. Okay, Mom likes bracelets. We need to think. What else does she like?

SHOW WHAT YOU LEARNED

Keith: Um, books, plants, bike rides, building stuff. Oh, and asking us if we want to learn carpentry, even though we always say no. She's pretty determined about that.

Agnes *(laughing)*: Yeah. I feel like she's been trying to get us to be interested for years now.

Keith: That's it. Coupons!

Agnes: Huh?

Keith: We can make coupons or vouchers that say we'll do whatever she wants. Even if it is not our favorite thing to do. So, if she gives us a coupon for an afternoon learning carpentry, we'll have to do it. I have paper and colored pencils in my room.

Scene 3: *In Agnes's still messy bedroom, a few days later. Agnes and Keith are sitting on the bed, playing a game. Mom enters.*

Mom: I really liked building with you. The coupons were a terrific gift. So terrific, that I'm going to use another one right now. *(The twins look with curiosity at each other and then at Mom.)* Agnes, I'd love to see the floor of your room. Hint, hint. *(hands Agnes a coupon)*

Agnes *(playfully groaning)*: Okay. A present is a present.

(Mom leaves and Agnes turns to Keith) Now I really wish I had found the bracelet!

Scene 4: *Agnes's room, a few hours later. Agnes is halfway done cleaning. Keith is helping. Agnes picks up a shoe to put away. The bracelet falls out. Keith, sighing, shakes his head. Agnes makes a silly face. The twins give a little laugh.*

1 In Scene 2, what can you infer from Agnes's reaction to Keith coming into the room?

A   She wants Keith to think she likes the book.

B   She is annoyed by him.

C   She doesn't want him to know the bracelet is missing.

D   She is tired of Keith saying her room is messy.

Quick Tip

It may help you to underline or circle key words in a question to better understand what it is asking.

2 What is the main theme of the play?

F   There can be more than one solution to a problem.

G   Everyone makes mistakes.

H   Helping others can make you feel good.

J   Learning new things can be surprisingly fun.

3 Why is there more than one scene in this play?

A   The twins have a backyard.

B   There is more than one character.

C   There are a lot of stage directions.

D   The setting and time change.

4 What does Agnes's dialogue in Scene 3 tell you?

F   She's happy her mother likes the present.

G   She wishes she didn't have to clean her room.

H   She wants Keith to help her clean.

J   She regrets giving her mother the coupons.

EXTEND YOUR LEARNING

HOMOGRAPHS

COLLABORATE

Homographs are words that are spelled the same but have different meanings and sometimes different pronunciations. **Homophones** are words that are pronounced the same but have different meanings and are often spelled differently. Words with different meanings but the same spelling and pronunciation are both homographs and homophones.

- Read the examples in the chart and say each homograph aloud. Think about how the meanings, pronunciations, and parts of speech differ.

- Add other homographs to the chart. Use a dictionary to find each word's meaning and part of speech and to compare pronunciation.

Homograph	Meaning 1	Part of Speech	Meaning 2	Part of Speech	Pronunciation of the Words
close	nearby	adjective	to shut	verb	different
hamper	to get in the way of progress	verb	a large basket with a cover	noun	same

TEXT STRUCTURE: PROBLEM AND SOLUTION

Authors sometimes use a problem-and-solution text structure to organize their writing. They describe problems and then explain how the problems were solved. On page 101 of "She Had to Walk Before She Could Run," the author states that Wilma Rudolph lost the use of her left leg after contracting polio. Then the author describes how this problem was solved as Rudolph underwent physical therapy and eventually regained the use of her leg.

Reread the rest of the biography on pages 102–103 and look for a problem-and-solution text structure. Then complete the chart below.

Problem	Solution

PRIMARY AND SECONDARY SOURCES

A **primary source** is an original record told by a firsthand witness to an event. It might be a letter, an interview, a diary, or other document. A **secondary source** is an account told by someone who was not present at the event. These resources include encyclopedias and textbooks.

Earlier in the unit, you read a biography of Wilma Rudolph. Research two additional facts about her. One fact should come from a primary source and one from a secondary source.

The primary source I used was: _____

Fact 1: _____

_____

The secondary source I used was: _____

Fact 2: _____

_____

On a separate piece of paper, write a bibliography with information about your sources.

- For **print** sources, include the author's last name and first name, the title of the source, the publisher's location, the publisher, and the year the source was published.

- For **online** sources, include the author's last name and first name, the website name, URL, publication date, and the date you accessed, or read, the source.

FIGURATIVE LANGUAGE

In "Dramatic Decisions: Theater Through the Ages" you read about the playwright William Shakespeare. We use many idioms today that appear in his works. Below are some idiomatic expressions from Shakespeare's plays and their meanings.

Phrase	Meaning	Example Sentence
all of a sudden	suddenly or not expected	All of a sudden, the sky turned gray and it started to rain.
good riddance	People say *good riddance* to express that they are happy someone or something is gone.	"Good riddance to all that noise," said my mother when the street work was finally finished.

Use print and digital sources to research other idiomatic expressions from Shakespeare's plays that we still use today. Fill in the chart, and then give other examples on a separate piece of paper.

Phrase	Meaning	Example Sentence

Pixtal/age Fotostock

TRACK YOUR PROGRESS

WHAT DID YOU LEARN?

Use the rubric to evaluate yourself on the skills you learned in this unit.
Write your scores in the boxes below.

4	3	2	1
I can successfully identify all examples of this skill.	I can identify most examples of this skill.	I can identify a few examples of this skill.	I need to work more on this skill.

☐ Author's Point of View   ☐ Idioms   ☐ Point of View

☐ Theme   ☐ Homophones   ☐ Figurative Language

Something that I need to work more on is _____ because

_____

_____

_____

Text to Self Think back over the texts that you have read in this unit.
Choose one text and write a short paragraph explaining a personal
connection that you have made to the text.

I made a personal connection to _____ because _____

_____

_____

_____

_____

Integrate RESEARCH AND INQUIRY

Present Your Work

Discuss with your partner how you will present your email to a volunteer organization that interests you. Use the Listening Checklist as your classmates give their presentations. Discuss the sentence starters below and write your answers.

While planning my presentation, I learned that email _____

_____

_____

Now I would like to know more about _____

_____

_____

Listening Checklist

☐ As you listen to the presentation, jot down any questions you have so that you will remember them later.

☐ Ask questions politely.

☐ Make sure your questions are relevant to the topic. If you don't understand the presenter's response, ask a follow-up question.

☐ Provide thoughtful feedback.

FatCamera/Getty Images